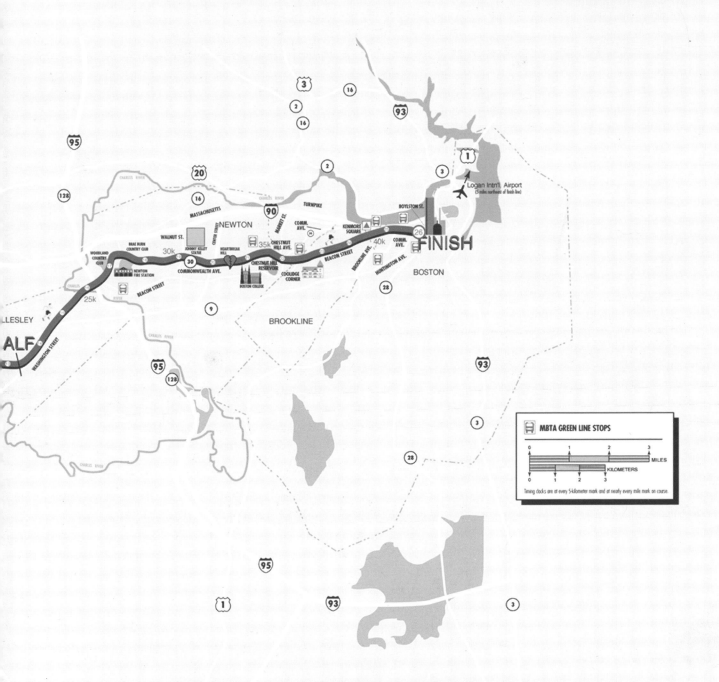

MBTA GREEN LINE STOPS

0   1   2   3   MILES

0   1   2   3   KILOMETERS

Timing clocks are at every 5-kilometer mark and at nearly every mile mark on course.

26 MILES TO BOSTON

26 MILES TO BOSTON

The Boston Marathon Experience from Hopkinton to Copley Square

Michael Connelly

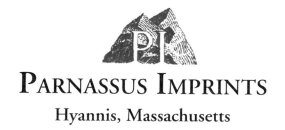

PARNASSUS IMPRINTS

Hyannis, Massachusetts

Parnassus Imprints
30 Perseverance Way
Hyannis, MA 02601

Library of Congress Catalog Card Number: 97-76269

Manufactured in Canada

With Love and Thanks

To my friends for their support and friendship
To my Nana Kenny who inspired me to write
To my Nana Connelly whose perpetual smile made a Sunday lunch a radiant experience
To my father-in-law, Tom Concannon, who showed me courage through a simple walk
To my siblings who aren't just my brothers and sisters but also my friends
To my parents for their love and guidance
To my wife, Noreen, and my son, Ryan, for filling my life with love and purpose

CONTENTS

FOREWORD

by John "Elder" Kelley

The Boston Marathon in its present form is the greatest Marathon in the world due to the guidance of the Boston Athletic Association (Guy Morse, Gloria Ratti and the other members of the BAA) and the John Hancock Financial Services Company (major sponsor), which now is a great help to the BAA. No other Marathon in the world can match the race for color, longevity, glamour, prestige and history. This is the race that the best runners in the world want to win even more than the Olympic Marathon (incidentally first prize is a lot more).

During the past twenty-five years or so women runners have been added to the race, who in my opinion are just as great athletes as the men. Women such as Joan Benoit can train for two or three years and run a 2:40 Marathon. Benoit is the two-time champion in the Women's Division. Someone once told me that the Wellesley College administration at one time did not allow the girls to watch the runners go by. How things have changed!

In 1921, at the age of 12, I was taken by my father to see my first Boston Marathon. At that race I saw Frank Zuna from New York come down Commonwealth Avenue and my father said, "Look at all the pep he has." I guess I fell in love with it then. I found out in later years that my mother said, "I never, ever dreamed that I would have a son who would run the Marathon."

The following pages enabled me to relive the race and its history. *26 Miles to Boston* and its different voices speak to both runners and fans. The book is unique in its ability to capture the Boston Marathon and marathoning itself. Through each chapter the reader can appreciate and feel the challenge of the athletic event while also getting a sense of the celebration over the course of the route.

As a spectator, two-time champion, 61-time participant and Grand Marshall of the race, I truly appreciate the number of perspectives represented in *26 Miles to Boston*. While reading the book, I reflected upon many wonderful experiences and found great pride in the fact that I have been part of something of such character and quality.

I'm proud to contribute to this book. I feel it truly captures the spirit, history and strategy of a wonderful athletic event. I hope you enjoy it as much as I did.

Best Wishes to Ron + Barbara Hawes
from
Johnny Kelley

Johnny Kelley
January 1998

FOREWORD

by Bill Rodgers

When Michael Connelly contacted me to write a bit about his book, *26 Miles to Boston,* I wasn't overly enthusiastic. It seemed to me that the race had received enough attention as it was. Was I wrong! Connelly writes about the old race from many new and interesting angles. You can't help but be seduced by this book. The stories flow one after another like a marathon runners' footsteps. Each story adds to the razzle dazzle of the race's long and colorful history.

Of course that's exactly what the Boston Marathon has to offer—lots of colorful history over the 101 years of the race. But no one has told the other stories of the race beyond those of the top runners. Connelly does give the other perspectives and thoughts, and I salute him for doing so, as it is only in recent days (as you'll see from reading the book) that the top runners have received respect as world class athletes. As recently as my win in 1975, a well known Boston sports commentator indicated that the runners at the Boston Marathon weren't athletes at all!

Because of my own background as a competitive runner, I've always been interested in reading about the top runners at the Boston Marathon and enjoyed the accounts of the race. People like Clarence DeMar, Johnny Kelley and Joan Benoit Samuelson have told of their exploits as champions at Boston. The top racers of the 90s have been of interest too, but what I truly enjoyed reading in *26 Miles to Boston* were the stories *never told*—accounts of volunteers, police officers, medical personnel, merchants in stores along the route, spectators, officials and of course the "average runner," such as Michael Connelly's account of his own race experience as an amateur runner fulfilling a promise to himself to run the Boston Marathon. The athlete's challenge is what the Boston Marathon is all about. The athlete's heart beats away inside all of us. Connelly writes, as he ran up Heartbreak Hill, "I noticed a man running with a prosthesis on one of his legs, thus causing me to be both inspired and proud to be part of an event where courage is just as important as athletic ability."

Having run the race 13 times, won four and dropped out of the race twice, I know what it feels like to take on the challenge of running the Boston Marathon. Michael Connelly does too, but he goes on to explore why a simple foot race has the impact it has on runners and non-runners alike. Some overly intellectual sedentary fellow once observed that runners never seem to smile as they run. Surely he was never at the Boston Marathon. Had he been, he would've seen real smiles, the ones with really deep satisfaction behind them.

To run the Boston Marathon is not an easy thing. To write well about it and explain its charisma is even harder. Michael Connelly's *26 Miles to Boston* is a winner in this regard. The reason I say this is that not many sports books have the capacity to make you feel as though the event was happening only ten feet away. This one does do that. Connelly has exposed the special qualities of the Boston Marathon foot race and why it is more than an ordinary sporting event.

Bill Rodgers
January 1998

FOREWORD

by Uta Pippig

For more than a century, the Boston Marathon has been a great race. No marathon in the world, including the Olympics, has the tradition, charm and character of Boston. The Boston Marathon is special because its history is so tangible. Because the original course and many great runners are still a part of the race, you can see and live a century of running. Each race adds to this legacy and enhances the allure of this wonderful event.

When I was a citizen of East Germany, I dreamed of running just one race—the Boston Marathon. I dreamed of just being a part of the race; to win seemed beyond my greatest expectations. I feel very fortunate to have been victorious in this great old marathon and rank my win in the 100th running as my most satisfying running achievement.

Many people make this race possible. The Boston Athletic Association does a wonderful job managing such a difficult event. Every runner is treated as an equal and each is able to run on the finely-tuned course. John Hancock Financial Services, the race's primary sponsor, provides the Boston Marathon the necessary financial support and guidance to continue into the next century. It is through the efforts of many that those involved in the event are made to feel like a family and a team.

Boston and the Boston Marathon compliment each other well. The city contributes immeasurable support while the marathon furnishes Boston with an event of exceptional quality. Both the city and the race are very special to me. I just love Boston! I feel as though the people of Boston have taken me in as one of their own. It's like my home away from home!

The fans who line the course have a wonderful understanding of the race and warm and sincere support for each runner. This is very special—they are as much a part of the race as the runners. I often wonder if other runners also feel a special connection with the spectators. Their overwhelming energy and support carry into other aspects of my life and draws me back to Boston. When I visit in the summer or in the autumn, I enjoy driving out to Hopkinton and Ashland, or running through Newton, or just walking the streets of Boston. I can feel the Boston Marathon even though the race is months away.

The history and important qualities of the Boston Marathon are chronicled well in *26 Miles to Boston*. The many opinions and stories provide a great perspective of the race. For those who are new to Boston, the book is an invitation to the race and its history. It is like a runner's personal handbook, providing a recipe on how to run a marathon. For race veterans, it serves as a memento, a reminder of Boston's great moments and extraordinary history.

In reading *26 Miles to Boston*, you will come to appreciate why this race is so loved around the world. Perhaps it will also give you a good feeling because it shows the Boston Marathon as a wonderful way for people to come together in peace and happiness, and in doing so, help to create another important chapter in the long and illustrious history of this great event.

Uta Pippig
January 1998

INTRODUCTION

To capture the essence of the Boston Marathon experience, one must live it, watch it, drink it and run it. Each perspective provides a unique look at why a simple road race has taken on the mantle of a legendary event.

The Boston Marathon is life itself. For a hundred years the Mecca of all running events has acted as a metaphor for the world around it. As the world has rotated and evolved, the Boston Marathon has evolved with it.

Each April, people from every corner of the world travel thousands of miles in order to travel 26 miles. No where on the face of the earth do more people from more diverse backgrounds gather for a one-day event. The Boston Marathon is a celebration of tradition, it is a celebration of health and fitness, it is a celebration of life. From Hopkinton to Boston, the spectators and runners are provided a stage on which to act out a play that stretches the gamut from Shakespeare to Pee Wee Herman. Tragedy, triumph, love, frustration and comedy are all components of this road race.

The 26 miles of roads, sidewalks and bridges are nothing more than a backdrop for athletic conquests, athletic failures, weddings, inebriated college students and over-priced vendors—all of whom play an intricate role in molding this race and its legacy.

The ultimate purposes of the Boston Marathon are as distinct as the people who embrace it. Whether your goal is to run, to barbecue, to say hello to your neighbor, to gather with your family or to delay studying for college finals, the race is a willing partner for all who come to celebrate.

When I contemplated the practicality of writing a book about the Boston Marathon, I was concerned with how many doors I could open considering the fact that I run 10-minute miles.

But thankfully, my concern dissipated the more I focused on the theme of the book. *26 Miles to Boston* is about the entire Boston Marathon experience. It's not a knock-down, black-and-white running book with lectures about carbohydrates, glycogen and running form. This book is written so that spectator, runner (amateur or professional), worker and volunteer can all appreciate their contributions to the race and at the same time gain a better understanding of the race's many and varied perspectives they have yet to experience.

With that in mind, I realized that my diverse experiences involving the Boston Marathon made me a worthy candidate to write a book of this sort. For almost a third of the race's history, I have had the pleasurable opportunity of witnessing the race from almost every angle possible. In the early years, I saw the race from my father's shoulders; in college, I watched the race from a keg party in an apartment that overlooked Cleveland Circle; after college, I cautiously stood on a rooftop just past Kenmore Square; years later, I took the baton from my father and provided shoulders for my own son; and finally, for the 100th running of the Boston Marathon, I celebrated the event by witnessing the race from the inside-out as a competitor—thus fulfilling my annual pledge that someday I would run Boston.

The following pages represent my attempt to capture the soul of the race in print. My ultimate goal is to bring the reader on a Marathon odyssey that captures the topographical uniqueness of each mile and the runner's experience as he or she traverses it. Throughout the book, the reader will be exposed to four distinct perspectives of the race and its history. The following list represents these four perspectives.

1. The first perspective is a narrative description of my experiences both as a runner and as a spectator. The narrative sections will be noted by *italicized* print and my initials *MPC*.

2. The second perspective will be historical anecdotes of the race. These facts will be noted by **bold** print and the year that the particular action happened, placed in a gray background.

3. The third viewpoint comes from the great runners of the race—their thoughts, remembrances and running strategies. These accounts, will try to give the reader a glimpse into the psyche's of the world's greatest runners, will be noted by *italicized* print.

4. The fourth perspective is a product of the insights of the many spectators, officials and business owners who line the course including mayors and selectmen, fire chiefs, police chiefs, real estate agents, historians, store owners and representatives from the three colleges, two country clubs and one hospital along the route. These viewpoints provide a look at the race from the outside-in, and are set in *italicized* print.

In my attempt to provide the reader with the quintessential look at the Boston Marathon experience, my labors would have been for naught if it weren't for a number of friends and associates who helped to make it all possible: my wife, Noreen Connelly, who was stuck driving the route, listening to me whine and providing encouragement for her spouse no matter how slow he ran or wrote; my mother, Marilyn Connelly, who has spent her life reading term papers, book reports and now manuscripts; my father, John J. Connelly, Jr. who is the ideal devil's advocate; Wallace Exman, my editor, who took a chance on me; Uta Pippig, whose grace, courage and athletic accomplishment qualify her as the ideal person to introduce this book and thus honor these pages with her thoughtful words; Johnny "The Elder" Kelley, whose two championships, seven second-place finishes, 18 top ten finishes and 58 overall finishes make him not only the patriarch of the race but also the perfect individual to help christen the book; four-time winner, Bill Rodgers who provided an eloquent introduction. Also: Dr. Maureen Connelly, Jack Fleming (special thanks), Gloria Ratti and Lars Dietrich of the Boston Athletic Association, Charlie Gaffney, Martin Duffy, Bruce Shaw, Angela Heffernan, Tom McLaughlin, Richard Twombly, Jack Radley, Tom Ratcliffe, John Cronin at the *Boston Herald*, Roy Clark, Chris Young, Dan Shaughnessy, Dorothy Deslongchamps of the Natick Historical Society, Dick Fannon of the Ashland Historical Society, Carolyn McGuire of the Framingham Historical Society, Susan Abele of the Newton Historical Society, Laura Nelson of the Wellesley Historical Society, Bob Sullivan of the Brookline Library, Becky Saletan, Aaron Schmidt and Charles Longley of the Boston Public Library, Tracy & Jeff McEvoy, Dr. Diane English (Orthopedic Surgeon), Dr. Caroline Foote (Cardiologist), Jennifer Worden and Sandra Southworth as well as physical therapists at the Prescription Orthopedic Sports Therapy clinic, my friends at Everett Savings Bank and a host of others whose ideas, imput and suggestions have all been incorporated into this project.

Thank you all for making this project a reality.

PART I

STRETCHING OUT

THE GENESIS

Helicopters hover over head; officials bark on two-way radios; trucks, capped with satellite dishes, fight for parking spaces; and a National Guard troop takes up a position as Hopkinton, Massachusetts prepares to host the start of another Boston Marathon. A century after the original starting line was drawn in the dirt down the road in Ashland, thousands of athletes "toe the line" as the clock approaches high noon.

For 364 days of the year, the sleepy colonial town of Hopkinton slowly rises to welcome each new morning. But today is the 365th day, and no matter how hard Hopkinton tries to hide its head deep under her pillow, it's impossible. This day is a day like no other. Today is the day of the Boston Marathon.

On this morning, the sounds of chirping birds are drowned out by a parade of shuttle buses; the smell of fresh-brewed coffee is overpowered by the aroma of muscle-soothing liniment; the knock on the door by a thrown newspaper is replaced with the knock of a total stranger requesting the use of your bathroom; the sight of squirrels re-acclimating themselves on the town green after a winter's hibernation is displaced by a scene of thousands and thousands of carbo-crazed, bladder-bursting contortionists all on this the 365th day.

This manifestation at Hopkinton is for the benefit of intellectually-challenged athletes who have chosen to abuse their bodies over the next two to five hours to the point that they will either be welcomed through the gates of Boston or the gates of St. Peter.

Decade after decade athletes of the highest level, if not the highest common sense, have ventured west of Boston in search of their Holy Grail. On this day, they will either push forward and conquer or sadly realize their physical and mental boundaries. They can't say no. Even though they understand the inevitable pain and anguish, they can't turn away. They are drawn by the awesome possibility of pushing beyond their imagined physiological limits. Through the streets of Boston and its suburbs, runners will throw themselves forward on an athletic journey of unparalleled peril.

The first train left the Boston & Albany Station, from Kneeland Street, at 7:00 A.M. and the second at 9:12 A.M. In all, fifteen runners made the trip to Ashland, with hopes of being the first of many who would attempt the implausible—a 25-mile run from Ashland to Boston.

*The trains dropped the runners and their attendants off in Ashland where they proceeded to the Central House Hotel for the pre-race dinner. The banquet hall was divided between two groups—the New York contingent on one side and the Boston and Cambridge runners on the other. The **Boston Globe** reported, on the morning of the race, "some of the runners are cracks from New York" and "these men are a fast set."*

After dinner, all runners were examined by a doctor in order to verify their capacity to withstand the arduous journey. Upon receiving a clean bill of health, the runners were then taken a mile up the road by a horse-drawn barge in order to toe the line. There, Tom Burke organized the fifteen runners on a makeshift starting line, which he drew by dragging his heel through the dusty road, raised his hand and yelled "GO!"

The idea for the Boston Marathon was hatched by two men back in 1896. John Graham, Boston Athletic Association (BAA) member and Harvard Track/United States Olympic coach, and his friend Herbert Holton, a financial agent out of Boston, ventured across the ocean to watch the 1896 Olympic Games in Athens. There, they witnessed a running event that pushed human physical limits. The event excited them so much that when they returned to Boston, they pledged to bring a similar sport to their city. Both men, true to their word, planned a route that would trace the trail of Paul Revere's ride from Boston to Concord.

Holton and Graham's effort to follow this historical route was nixed because the bridge from Boston to Cambridge was closed for repairs. So the two originators decided to let the ocean breezes of the Atlantic Ocean lead them.

With a Veeder cyclometer in hand, they pedaled out the gate of the Irvington Oval race track onto Huntington Avenue in Boston, down Exeter Street, past the BAA clubhouse, on to Commonwealth Avenue and then followed alongside the Boston/Albany train tracks, which they used as a guide. This route was ideal because railroad engineers were using the most advanced technology with regard to maps, laying tracks, direct routes, and tracking distances.

They pedaled and pedaled through town after town. From Boston, into Brookline, past Boston College, over the hills of Newton, through Wellesley, past Natick, over the train tracks of Framingham and into Ashland. At this point, Graham's cyclometer read 25 miles while Holton's read 24.5 miles. Holton continued down the road, and stopped when his cyclometer hit the 25-mile mark. He got off his bike, grabbed two rocks, and declared that very spot as the start of the first Marathon—a quiet dirt road called Pleasant Street, across from Metcalf's Mill, one mile from Ashland Center. Nowadays, the fact that the race started in Ashland isn't popular with the people of Hopkinton.

Ashland hosted the start of the race from 1887 to 1923. The start was eventually moved down the road to Hopkinton in 1924 in an effort to comply with the accepted Olympic distance of twenty-six miles, three hundred and eighty-five yards which was established during the 1908 Olympic Games in England. This was done to appease a spoiled king. Originally the length at the Olympic games had been determined by the distance between the Greek cities of Marathon and Athens. King Edward VII wanted the race to start at Windsor Castle and to finish in front of his royal box in the Olympic Stadium. So the King did what kings do. He issued a proclamation. "Here

The initial Boston Marathon was designed to duplicate an endurance event which was run at the 1896 Olympiad in Athens, Greece. That event was created in order to honor the trek of Pheideppides, the declarer of victory in 500 B.C. who ran from Marathon, Greece to Athens, Greece.

ळळळळळ

The Boston Marathon is run each year on the Massachusetts holiday of Patriot's Day. This is the day that commemorates the famous ride of Paul Revere and the battles in Lexington and Concord that ignited the American Revolution. Patriot's Day is widely celebrated throughout the state with many events including battle re-enactments, replays of Paul Revere's ride, Boston Red Sox baseball games at Fenway Park and, of course, the Boston Marathon.

ळळळळळ

Five-time wheelchair champion, Jim Knaub, described the Boston Marathon. "It is a race which is not competed against other athletes but raced against a supreme being. The Boston Marathon is bigger than life. It's a feeling like no other."

ye, here ye, here ye. The Marathon will start at Windsor Castle, and end in front of my seat, in the royal box, at the stadium thus making the official distance of the race twenty-six miles, three hundred and eighty-five yards. Therefore I don't have to get off my royal butt to see the race!" (Poetic license)

So in 1924, sixteen years after the distance was changed, the BAA moved the race to Hopkinton in order to adhere to the accepted length.

For a century, the history of the Marathon has been cultivated, nurtured and accommodated by individuals such as King Edward VII, Henry Holton and John Graham in order to provide a sporting event in which athletes defy limitations to meet the challenge and to honor Pheideppides, the first marathon runner.

So, with the train tracks on one side and Boston due east, runners continue to toe the line in solidarity with their many brothers and sisters, past and present, who have come to pay homage to the Mecca of all marathons.

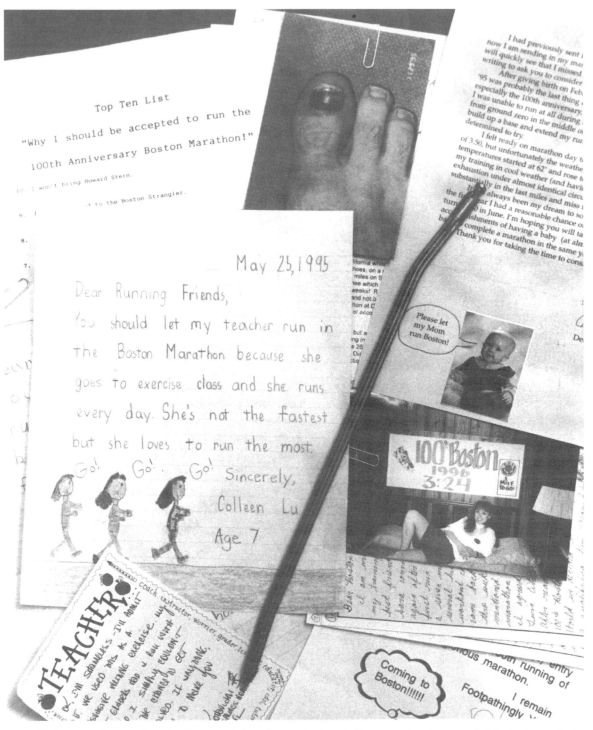

Non-qualifying applicants for the Boston Marathon tried to influence the Boston Athletic Association by sending letters, pictures and even a metal rod which was removed from a runner's leg during surgery. Photo courtesy of the *Boston Herald*.

MARATHON YEAR

MPC: Six months before the 100th running of the Boston Marathon, my exercise regime was limited to a run up and down a basketball court. This form of exercise, which included an occasional fifteen-footer between turn-overs, was sufficient enough to convince myself that I was staying active.

During a break between one of those pickup games, my friends Michael (Rad) Radley and Rich (Richie) Twombly joined me in a casual discussion about our shared aspiration to run a marathon someday. The tone of the conversation was more consistent with a throwaway line like, "I'd love to parachute someday" or "Would you ever bungee jump?" But for some reason, this throwaway line snowballed and before I knew it I found myself stretching out on my front porch in preparation for my first step towards the finish line in Boston.

One mile later, I gratefully arrived back at my house breathing heavily with tight hamstrings and a cramp in my side. It wasn't going to be easy.

But I was hooked. I gave Richie and Rad my word that I'd do it and there seemed to be no turning back. But, just in case I got an inclination to forego the jaunt for a more sedentary Patriot's Day, I made a point of telling every friend and family member I could that I was running the 100th in April. This way there was no out. I was stuck.

The race, which was originally identified as the American Marathon of the Boston Athletic Association is known throughout the world as the granddaddy of all marathons. Runners come from all corners of the world for the privilege of running "Boston."

Kathy Switzer, eight-time competitor and now television commentator, considered her runs in Boston as spiritual-athletic experiences. "To push yourself, and consider yourself a runner, you must make the pilgrimage to the Mecca. That's how important Boston is to runners. It's a religious experience.

"At the same time, it's an amazing opportunity to compete in the same arena with the best athletes in the world no matter your talent level. Imagine being able to shoot baskets with Larry Bird or skate with Bobby Orr—it's the same thing."

Over the last century the number of athletes entering the Boston Marathon has increased from 15 to over 40,000. This explosion of participants has forced the race's organizers, the BAA, to evolve from a cozy few, with one phone and a shoebox office, into an army of professionals with the responsibility of administering the greatest race of all.

Race management is an ongoing function. Each year, the BAA plans, administers and oversees the race only to have the whole cycle start all over again as soon as the last runner crosses the finish line. At that time, the planning and arguing begins for the subsequent year's race. Committees from each town throughout the route make adjustments, and sweat through nightmares of six-foot blizzards and bursting water pipes that might occur minutes before the race—eighteen inches of snow fell on Hopkinton just before the 1996 race.

Everything about the Boston Marathon is unique, including the route which moves through eight different towns from start to finish. Because of this, the coordination of logistics and the appeasement of the many voices are major undertakings. The different concerns and different requests of each town and each committee need to be resolved before April. If one town backed out of the race, the continuity of the world's oldest race would be disturbed forever.

The duty of playing host to tens of thousands of runners and officials can be a Herculean task for some of these rural towns. For example, on the 100th running of the race, 45,000 numbered and non-numbered (bandit) runners from over 70 countries lined up in Hopkinton. Add to that mix, spectators, race officials and fried dough salesmen, and the town grew from 13,505 (estimated population) to over 75,000 in one day.

The race's growing effect on the town and populace of Hopkinton is measurable. In 1915 the *Boston Globe* wrote, "Throughout the forenoon the little square in the town resembled a scene in the country on a main railroad line that had been honored by a circus." The huge 1966 entry list of 540 names provoked some Hopkinton officials to request that the BAA restrict the next year's enrollment to invitation only. In 1984, because of budgetary constraints within the town, a contingency of Hopkinton residents initiated a petition to move the race out of town.

Similar financial concerns in 1996 induced the town of Hopkinton to auction off the pace car, sell marathon quilts, build a corporate box at the starting line and create a special marathon wine—a concoction which the *Boston Globe* noted "suggests the aroma of sneakers, might give you the runs and starts strong but wilts." Following the race that year, as compensation for hosting the race and pre-race activities, Hopkinton High School received a new track and newly-seeded and lighted field hockey, soccer and baseball fields.

For the 101st running of the Marathon in 1997, it was the BAA's intention to reduce the field to 15,000 from the over 40,000 in 1996. "We made commitments to the communities of Hopkinton and Boston that we would go back to a reasonable field size which is more representative of what is typical Boston," said Guy Morse of the BAA. The fee for running the race was $75 for runners from the United States and $100 for all others.

Many of these concerns have since been alleviated with the marriage between the Boston Athletic Association and its financial sponsor in 1986. At that time, the BAA and John Hancock Financial Services entered into an arrangement which provided the necessary monetary support for the race to survive and prosper. Under this agreement, each town was provided with a stipend to help defray the costs incurred in hosting the race. This greatly improved the relationship between the towns and the BAA, and between budget committees and their town selectmen. The Hancock and the BAA are currently in the middle of a 15-year contract worth $18,000,000 which extends into the next century.

Four-time winner Bill Rodgers recently reflected on the Marathon and its history. "The marriage between John Hancock and the Boston Marathon is the most significant event since the origin of the race. This sponsorship

SPONSORS AND THE RESPECTIVE VALUE OF THEIR SERVICES OR DONATIONS FOR THE 1996 BOSTON MARATHON.

$1.4 m
- John Hancock Financial Services, Inc.

$400m to $500m
- Adidas of America, Inc.
- Citgo Petroleum Corporation

$100m to $200m
- Belmont Springs Water Company, Inc.
- Digital Equipment Corporation
- Gatorade/Quaker Oats Company, Inc.
- Northwest Airlines
- Pontiac
- Ronzoni/Hershey Pasta
- Tylenol

$30m to $75m
- AT&T
- Boston Gas
- *Boston Phoenix*
- CellularOne
- CVS
- Filenes
- Longs Jewelers/RJC Company
- Ocean Spray Cranberries, Inc
- Offtech Inc.
- Powerbar/Powerfood Inc.
- Sunshine Biscuits

allows the race to head towards its second century while maintaining the highest degree of quality and sportsmanship possible."

In 1905, it cost the BAA a total of $1,326 to run and organize the tenth Marathon. Over following years, the BAA took $2,500 from the proceeds of its popular indoor track event in order to fund the race. In its struggle to finance the 1933 Marathon, the BAA called for sponsors to assist in planning and funding the race. The organization claimed that it was going to end the Marathon unless it got help from the newspapers and the local Chamber of Commerce. The budget for the 1981 Marathon equaled $45,000.

Contributions by sponsors represented $3.6 million in 1996. This income plus $1.9 million from entry fees and $400,000 from royalties was used to offset the $5.9 million cost of the race.

Adrian Leek, of Adidas America, Inc., felt fortunate that his company could get involved with an event such as the Boston Marathon. "To be able to link with an event like the Boston Marathon provides our company with instant credibility. To formulate a relationship with a health and fitness celebration of this magnitude, which is held in such high regard throughout the world for its tradition, class and quality is a marketing dream. The exposure our company receives is national and international. Events like this are few and far between."

While committees, sponsors, athletic associations and local residents bang heads and iron out differences of opinion ("What do those people in Boston know anyway?"), fire chiefs, police chiefs and package store owners from the eight towns gather to coordinate their own song and dance. Safety rules, alternative routes, overtime budgets and price increases on kegs of beer are all important issues which must be straightened out long before the starter's gun scares some of Hopkinton's birds.

Somehow, all of these problems and concerns right themselves just in time for the race, thanks to the directions of the BAA.

The Boston Athletic Association was founded in the 1880s. Its clubhouse, which is no longer in existence, was located on Exeter Street in Boston, the current location of the Boston Public Library's Johnson Building, where the finish line was located from 1899 to 1964 before being switched to Boylston Street. Men like John Graham, George Brown, Walter Brown, Jock Semple, Will Cloney and Guy Morse have all been worthy representatives of both the BAA and the race that they hold so near and dear.

As the year's cycle continues and the BAA puts out the endless fires which spark from town to town, their other duties continue to mount. Housing for the elite runners must be arranged, press accommodations must be finalized, applications from non-qualifying runners must be fielded.

Jack Fleming is responsible for the daunting task of media and public relations. Considering that the BAA issues more press credentials for this one-day sporting event than any other one-day event in the world except for the Superbowl, Jack's plate is full throughout the year.

The presence of the media as we know it today began in 1928 when WEEI provided radio coverage for the first time including musical interludes from the Daily Maide. Hollywood entered the picture in 1941 when runners lined up on the starting line and ran a mock start before the race in order to provide footage for the Movietone cameras. In 1949, TV coverage was provided for the first time with live shots sent to living rooms from Kenmore Square and the finish line. The television arm of the Public Broadcasting System covered the 1979 race in its entirety for the first time. The race was shown in tape delay. Kathy Switzer, a past competitor, was one of the commentators. "We drove the course in golf carts in the freezing cold. After a half-hour of footage, we would take the tape and throw it from the course over the crowd of spectators to a waiting PBS employee. He would then deliver it to the press truck for showing."

The BAA handed out press credentials to over 1,500 journalists from 350 media outlets covering the 1996 race.

Barbara Sicuso of the BAA has the job of fielding requests from non-qualifying applicants which is always an interesting, if not heart-wrenching, duty. In 1996 there were 30,000 rejections. Each year the requests to run Boston become more creative. The bad breaks or self-diagnosed diseases that prevented applicants from running a qualifying marathon earlier in the year stagger the imagination.

Dennis Rainear had always dreamed of running the Boston Marathon. In order to qualify for the 1976 race, Rainear needed to run the Grand Valley Marathon in Allendale, Michigan in a time of three hours or better. His previous best had been 3:00:31. As he passed the ten-mile mark, he felt a thud on the side of his head. He looked around to see who had thrown what he thought was a brick but he saw no one. Rainear, although somewhat dazed, couldn't afford to waste any time. So, he continued to the finish in three hours and nine minutes.

Hours later, Rainear went to a local hospital to have his pounding headache examined. There, a doctor discovered that the runner had been shot in the head by a twenty-two caliber rifle. After the examination, Rainear met the press who were swarming all over him after hearing his story. At the impromptu press conference, Rainear remarked that he failed to qualify for Boston because he had a hole in his head.

When the story was brought to the attention of the BAA, they made a rare exception and provided Dennis Rainear with a number for the 1979 Boston Marathon.

The Rainear incident was one of the few requests to escape the BAA's barrel, although some requests certainly deserve a second look. A 1992 request for a number came from a depressed wife of a perspective marathoner. She pleaded, "Either you give my husband a number or I'll be divorced or widowed because if he doesn't run I won't be able to live with him!" In 1995, an applicant claimed that he deserved a number because of his uncanny resemblance to Abraham Lincoln. He provided a life-size cardboard cut-out of himself with his request. He was denied.

With a week to go, applications have either been accepted or denied. Most of the press have been issued their credentials and each town's requests have been answered and hopefully satisfied. The hard work of the BAA and the runners will soon come to fruition.

Members of the Korean contingency (L-R manager Sohn Kee Chung, Song Kil Yoon, Hann Kil Yong and Choi Yan Chil) arrive at Logan Airport for the 1950 Boston Marathon.
Photo courtesy of the *Boston Herald*.

MARATHON WEEK

Over the last hundred years the Marathon has blossomed from a half-day event to an entire week of Marathon madness. Early in the week, the elite runners from around the world begin to arrive. In the early years of the race before professional athletes and appearance of money, the runners were left to their own devices to get to Boston. Some would hobo from train to train, while others were forced to hitchhike rides. But one way or another their crusade was for a good cause.

As the elite athletes from around the world start to arrive in Boston, they begin to reap benefits that are usually bestowed upon kings and queens. The runners are picked up at the airport by assigned volunteers provided by the BAA and John Hancock Financial Services. They are then delivered to their home away from home at the John Hancock Conference Center which is just yards away from the finish line. This makeshift Olympic Village, which is usually reserved for the captains of industry, is now reserved for these long distance harriers. There are 64 suites and a recreation room, which is decorated appropriately with the paintings of the patriarch of the race, John Kelley, who is a two-time winner and a 61-time participant.

Here the runners eat what they want, when they want. Ethiopian specialty? They have it. Beef stroganoff? No problem. Knockwurst and sauerkraut? "Coming up." All food is prepared as ordered and served according to the different time zones of the runners. The runners are also provided with masseuse service by members of the American Massage Therapy Association in order to loosen and calm sore and tense muscles. A movie room is available with a full video library (comedies are the most desired films). Tickets for Boston sporting events such as the Celtics, Bruins and Red Sox are on hand—all in attempt to provide your basic Boston hospitality.

Three-time champion Cosmas Ndeti acts as his own chef when he arrives on the Thursday before the race. Cosmas concocts a dish called Ugaali, his favorite meal, which is white corn meal complemented with a soup-like mixture of chicken, onions, tomatoes, greens and carrots.

For soothing his muscles he utilizes the manipulating fingers of Kati Touminen, the wife of Nike employee Jaakko Touminen.

International runners who are new to the race are always anxious to the see the route, especially Heartbreak Hill. As their fellow countrymen and women return each year from past Marathons, the legend of "the hills" grows and grows.

In order to see if these hills are really as high as the Himalayas, the runners arrange to have volunteers drive them out to see the course.

As rookies review the route from Hopkinton to Boston, it can be a bit of a letdown when they finally see the hills. The stories from the past runners led them to believe that a competitor needs a rope to scale these legendary monsters, but instead they simply appear to be three inclines between the starting line and the finish. But, as is the case of Niagara Falls, until you go over the Falls in a barrel, they don't look that bad either.

On Thursday, Tommy Leonard of the old Eliot Lounge, the race's unofficial watering hole and better described by some as the throbbing heart of the Marathon, raises the race flags inside the bar (which stands at the 26-mile mark), to officially kick off the bash. This is the perfect excuse for runners and non-runners to get a jump on their carbo-loading.

Tommy Leonard has been described by some as the Archbishop of the Boston Marathon while others have called him the Guru. But whatever he is called, Tommy loves the Boston Marathon and takes advantage of every opportunity to wax poetic on the race which is so beautifully personified by the man whose side job is drawing beer taps at the Eliot Lounge. His full-time job for 25 years was to provide a metaphoric, passionate, analytic history and divination on the beauty and purpose of the race which he passionately embraces, and which he personally has conquered over 20 times himself. His best time was 3:17 in 1975.

In the autumn of 1996 the Eliot Lounge was closed, forcing the 63-year-old bartender to find another home for himself and the thousands of marathoners who considered the Eliot Lounge as much a part of the race as Heartbreak Hill. Leonard could only say, "I'm laughing on the outside but crying on the inside."

1976. **A week before the Marathon, Jack Fultz wrote to his friend Jerry: "I just have this good feeling. Something big is going to happen next week." A week later he was crowned champion of the Boston Marathon.**

1996. **Cosmas Ndeti received a letter from a fellow born-again Christian from Germany. In the letter, the writer stated that he had a dream in which Cosmas won the Boston Marathon with a time of 2:06:38. Amazingly, this was the time Ndeti had projected in his running log. Ndeti now felt he was destined to win his fourth Boston and smash the world record in the 100th running.**

1913. **It took William Kennedy, affectionately known as "Bricklayer Bill," five days to make it from Chicago to Boston in order to run in the Marathon. Kennedy, who won the championship in 1917, was forced to jump from freight train to freight train in order to make the trip. In the past, a local company had paid his way to run Boston. But this year Kennedy had been stricken with typhoid fever. This led the benefactor to shy away, feeling Kennedy would be unable to contend for the championship.**

1977. **Frank Shorter, the 1972 Olympic champion, was asked why he wouldn't run Boston. He complained, "I'm not going to hitchhike to Boston." Race coordinator Will Cloney retorted, "He knows there is a little 'angel' (a silent financial benefactor) available to provide the trip to Boston."**

1993. In an effort to provide the most hospitable environment possible for the athletes, BAA officials presented three-time champion Ibrahim Hussein with a waffle maker, an electric converter, and several boxes of waffle mix when he mentioned that he was unable to get waffles back home in Kenya.

1929. Two-time winner Johnny Miles was asked by the press if he was going to drive the course before the race. He answered, "Why, I'll see enough of it tomorrow."

1949. In an attempt to orient himself to the Marathon route, Swedish runner Karl Gosta Leandersson ran the course in record time 10 days before the race. Although he was pleased with his effort, Leandersson injured his Achilles tendon. On race day, the runner ignored the pain and won the race by more than three minutes.

1996. For the 100th running of Boston, Marathon Tours, Inc. provided a two-hour sightseeing trip over the length of the course. During the tour, there were quizzes, prizes and photo opportunities at famous landmarks along the route.

1997. One of the women's favorites, Fatuma Roba of Ethiopia, was asked at the pre-race press conference if she were going to view the course before the race. She answered, "I don't like to see the race place." She further stated, "I am very sure I will win. You have an American girl, a German girl who is good, a Russian, all these are my competitors. But I know I will beat them." Roba was later proved correct.

In September of 1997, the Back Bay Brewing Company, which is situated near the finish line, dedicated a room to Tommy, thus giving him a Marathon home in which to hang his Mylar blanket.

The weekend arrived and every hotel within 50 miles of the course had a "No Vacancy" sign hung in front. It was estimated that the 100th running of the Boston Marathon would generate $114 million for the Boston area economy.

After the 1996 race, the estimate was raised to $140 million in generated income. Biba's, a local hot spot restaurant, served 300 dinners on the Saturday night before the race, more than than they had ever served in a single day in their seven year existence. Below is a breakdown of the $140,110,000 of revenue which was generated as a function of the Boston Marathon.

> United States runners and guests $49.33
> Massachusetts runners $1.48
> International runners and guests $28.05
> Spectators and visitors along the course $42.81
> Media $1.3
> Transportation $11.66
> Prize money $ .6
> Maintenance of course $.9
> Impact of Sports and Fitness Expo $3.9
>   **Total $140.11 million**

Families throughout Massachusetts host competitors in an effort to create good will and to add hospitality to the overall experience. One resident of Hopkinton, who is a veteran of Fort Bragg in North Carolina, gives back to his old duty station by hosting runners currently stationed there.

Bob Nichol from Sharon, Massachusetts, a local wheelchair competitor, has hosted a fellow wheelchair competitor from South Africa for the last several years.

This veteran of the wars in South Africa travels halfway across the world to visit his Massachusetts friend to compete and fulfill a dream.

On the Thursday night before the 1988 race, John Treacy of Ireland, one of the world's premier marathon runners, rolled over in bed, and told his wife that he decided that he was going to win Boston. After leading the race in mile 21, he fell back to finish third running a 2:09:15

"I was convinced I could win the Boston Marathon. I had a great week of running and felt I was as prepared as I could be. It just so happens that Ibrahim Hussein and Juma Ikangaa pulled away and then worked together leaving me alone to work by myself. I knew I'd run well and sometimes that's enough."

Saturday and Sunday (and Friday for the 100th) are big days for the Sports and Fitness Expo at the John Hynes Convention Center on Boylston Street just a few city blocks from the finish line. The Expo started in the 70s on a folding table at the local YWCA, and has grown as the race has grown. The Expo provides a running smorgasbord for runners and their families as they prepare for the race on Monday. Here you can buy running footwear which do everything but move themselves. Some flash, some pump, some caress but for sure they all look better at the exhibit booth, than they do at mile 26. Along with the variety of promotional booths and islands (whose costs range between $2,000 and $16,600), there are several running and health clinics and seminars on subjects such as the "Boys of Boston," running your best, the future of running shoes, a medical Q&A, all of which are offered throughout the day to running aficionados.

Sunday afternoon provides towns along the route with the opportunity to gear up for the Marathon by providing racing activities for their townspeople. On Sunday morning, the city of Boston hosts the International Friend-

1996. In honor of the 100th running of the Boston Marathon, the City of Boston paid tribute to the past winners of the race by dedicating the Boston Marathon Monument in Copley Square Park on Tuesday of Marathon Week. In conjuction with the dedication of the monument, the BAA also presented Roberta Gibb and Sara Mae Berman with championship medals to commemorate their wins through the years 1966-1971. Along with the medals, their status as "unofficial" winners was reversed and is now listed as official.

1996. Over 90,000 running buffs attended the Expo and were treated to a runner's paradise by 100 exhibitors. Two of the more visible exhibitors were Adidas and Nike. As these two footwear giants fought for prime spacing and market share, they tried to catch the eye of the consumers by pushing free posters (commemorating the 100th running), $200 coats, sweat suits, socks and gloves, all in an effort to move product and grab a larger percentage of the runners' discretionary income.

1996. When it was discovered that many runners were without lodging before the race, the citizens of Hopkinton opened their doors to these athletes. In the end, lodging was provided for all.

1993. On the Saturday before the 97th running of the Boston Marathon, Cosmas Ndeti's wife gave birth to their first child. Two days later, Ndeti won his first of three Marathons and punctuated the significance of the Boston Marathon in his life by naming his boy Boston.

ship Run and a parade of former Marathon champions. In the afternoon, the town of Newton holds a similar event called the Heartbreak Hill International Youth Race which includes a family fun walk. On Saturday, Wellesley throws its own party, the Wellesley Community Children's Center Fun Run.

On the Sunday night before the race, the runners are treated to a pasta dinner worthy of a Marathon of this stature. The first pasta dinner for the runners was started back at the Eliot Lounge in the early 1980s. For a dollar you could stuff yourself sick. Now, dozens of restaurants and hotels in the vicinity of the course throw a mini version of the pasta festival which is now held at the World Trade Center in Boston.

In 1985 Image Impact, of New York, came to Boston in order to organize the pre- and post-race activities. They looked forward to the good-natured Boston racing crowd and the family atmosphere of the race. For the 100th running, Micky Lawrence of Image Impact estimated that the crowd would be in excess of 20,000 people at the annual pasta dinner.

In order to feed such a large family, Image Impact must do some serious shopping. Here is a peek at their shopping list:

- 3000 pounds of pasta
- 2500 pounds of lasagna noodles
- 350 gallons of sauce
- 1500 pounds of salad
- 1000 dozen rolls

Leftovers were donated to the local food banks for the hungry. The crowd at the 1996 pasta dinner was estimated at 20,000 runners and family members, the largest pasta dinner ever on Marathon weekend.

MPC: In an attempt to participate in the 100th running of the Boston Marathon, I left no stone unturned in my effort to obtain a number for the race. I called race sponsors, the BAA, politicians in each town and running clubs. I offered money, pathetic excuses and every sob story I could think of, but I still came up empty. I even called our local politician Maura Henningan, who had broken her foot in a car accident, and sadistically asked if I could use her number. Also to no avail.

So with six months of hard training under my belt, I was forced to run as a bandit with my training partners Michael and Jack Radley, and Rich Twombly.

As bandits, we were forced to find lodging in Hopkinton the night before the race because the roads into the town would be shut down to the public at 6:30 A.M. the next day. Luckily, family friends Jeff and Tracy McEvoy opened their doors to the four of us.

We drove out to their house around 10:00 on Sunday night. As we moved across the Marathon route, I felt electricity in the air—like a mixture between Christmas Eve as a child and the night before an execution on death row. With marathon signs and posters hanging from houses and campers on the side of road, there was a quiet so loud that it caused a premature flow of adrenaline. In fourteen hours, we would discover the magic of the Boston Marathon.

Uta Pippig works her way through the Congregational Church Cemetery toward the starting line in 1996.
Photo courtesy of Tim DeFrisco.

MARATHON DAY

By Monday morning, all the pasta has been eaten, Cheers' T-shirts have been bought and new sneakers tried on for size. It is time to go out and run the Boston Marathon.

Beginning at four o'clock in the morning, residents of Hopkinton begin to claim spots in the town center for the ideal vantage point from which to view the start.

At six o'clock, the Hopkinton Lions Club begins serving breakfast at their annual pancake feast. Proceeds go towards college scholarships for local residents.

MPC: Because of the excitement of the coming day's events, my sleep wasn't as sound as usual. I woke up around six o'clock, climbed out of my sleeping bag and made my way to the kitchen. No one else was awake so I was left alone with my thoughts. "Did I train enough? Would we be allowed to enter the race even though we didn't have a number? Would my knee hold up? What was I doing here?"

The longest race I had ever run was a 10K, only a quarter of what I would attempt on this day. Everything about this day was foreign to me. I was out of my element and I knew it.

For almost an hour I sat at Tracy and Jeff's kitchen table and contemplated my fate and my six month commitment. My ultimate fear was failure. Six months of pain and energy would be completely wasted if I pulled up on some sidewalk in Newton or Brookline. Sure, people would pat me on the back, and my family would tell me that I was a "winner in their book." But I was well aware of the ramifications of failure. Future challenges would be approached with doubt and hesitation. The ability to attack would be replaced with a degree of tentativeness which doesn't allow a person to realize his/her fullest potential. To fail or succeed today would result in subtle and not-so-subtle consequences reaching far beyond a tangible finish line.

Three-time Boston Marathon champion Uta Pippig's pre-race breakfast doesn't differ much from any of her other morning repasts. I want this day to be like any other day. Maybe I'll increase my carbohydrates slightly but the more this day begins like any other day, the more likely I'll be relaxed and ready to run at my peak."

At seven o'clock, the first shuttle bus leaves Copley Square for the ride to Hopkinton. The one and a half hour trip is filled with anxiety and apprehension. Some of the competitors nervously chatter amongst themselves while others, like seven-time winner Jean Driscoll, withdraw with their Walkmans to focus on their mission ahead. Others, like Jim Knaub, bundle up and take a nap.

Decades ago, the Tebeau family from Hopkinton, who from 1924–1965 hosted the start of the race at their farm, would have the cows milked and locked up by seven o'clock in order to prevent injury both to the cows and the runners.

By the time the first shuttle bus arrives in Hopkinton, Mugs Away Pub, at the seven-mile mark in Framingham, serves the first beer of the day in a race of another kind.

The town of Hopkinton is closed to all traffic at 6:30 A.M. except for the shuttle buses and vendors. Competitors meet at the Hopkinton High School, 1,000 yards from the start, in order to be assigned corrals for the start, dress or simply stay warm. The BAA tries to keep the athletes occupied with slide shows, music and massages. For the 100th running, the Japanese contingent requested their own tent to cater to their large number of runners—1355. The largest international representation was from Canada with 1,982 numbered competitors. California had the largest showing from any state outside of Massachusetts with 2,828.

In the past, runners met at various sites including the Central House, Columbia House, Ashland Hotel, Tebeaus' Farm and nearby Hopkinton Community building before winding up at the high school gym. These facilities provided sites for the runners to undergo physical examinations to demonstrate their ability to complete the long haul. In recent years, physical examinations have been canceled because the size of the running field makes it logistically impossible to administer the tests.

The last shuttle leaves Boston at ten o'clock. If you miss that one, you probably won't be running the race. As the clock rolls up to eleven o'clock, the runners start meandering down to the town common to stretch out.

1996. Head pancake flipper Jimmy Dumas makes his contribution to the day by cooking over 3,000 pancakes at the Lions Club Breakfast.

❧ ❧ ❧ ❧ ❧

1962. Four BAA officials, driving out to the start, were involved in a serious car crash. Their beach wagon flipped over two times before the vehicle settled. One man was thought to have a fractured skull while the other three were released in time to see the finish with injuries that required a back brace and eye patch.

1996. In an effort to transport more than 35,000 runners to the starting line, some of the 700 shuttle buses were backed up for hours, forcing fluid-binging runners to urinate into bottles while on the bus.

❧ ❧ ❧ ❧ ❧

1996. Because of the blizzard that hit Massachusetts the week of the Marathon, the town of Hopkinton was covered in mud. In an attempt to keep the facilities dry, the town placed Astroturf on the high school athletic fields where the runners gathered. A number of runners wore plastic bags over their sneakers in an effort to keep their footwear dry.

1903. Runner John Lorden received his physical before he went out to Ashland. The doctor told him, "If you run, your bowel problems could kill you." When Lorden arrived in Ashland for the start, he hid the doctor's note in his pocket and told the doctor on the scene that his physical was all set. They passed him his number and he ended up winning the race.

1908. Doctors issued a statement prior to the race. "Wind, race and the proper handling of stimulants will all be factors in the race."

1958. Runners John Lafferty, Ted Corbitt and Al Confalone (all of whom had run the race before), were ruled ineligible to run because doctors diagnosed each with heart murmurs. All three runners ran the race anyway by starting twenty-five yards behind the other competitors. They ended up finishing sixth, seventh and ninth respectively, but were not recognized by the BAA.

1973. Dr. Thomas Kelley administered pre-race physicals as he had been doing since 1931.

❦ ❦ ❦ ❦ ❦

1996. In Hopkinton, the BAA provides the runners with the world's largest urinal and more than five hundred portable potties in order to provide ample depositories for the hordes of bladder weary runners.

On the bandstand, the middle and high school bands help you concentrate with the strum and blow of each high note.

Jogging around the common, Rob Phipps of the Hopkinton Athletic Association keeps an eye on one of his many responsibilities—the positioning of the valuable, portable bathrooms. Throughout the year, many important issues have been coordinated, but none are more important than the placement of these facilities relating to two important facility fun facts—spillage and tonnage. With this in mind, the town has put great emphasis upon the positioning of these receptacles in areas on level ground that is not downwind.

MPC: As the clock ticked down to race time, Rad, Richie, Jackie and I finished breakfast and started to get dressed at Jeff and Tracy's house. For breakfast, we had toast with jam or peanut butter, bagels, oranges and bananas. While slugging the first of many liters of fluid, it came to my attention that I hadn't drunk with such passion since my senior week in college. Little did I know that at the end of this event I would feel very much as I did at the conclusion of my college career. While each of us took a turn in the bathroom, the others surrounded the television set to watch the pre-race festivities. We watched the shuttle buses arrive at the high school to drop off its load of muscle-cramped riders. As the cameras scanned the grounds of the high school, the landscape's resemblance to Woodstock made our stay with friends a warm and dry blessing.

As we continued to get ready, it seemed as if we were more likely embarking on a CIA survival mission than a simple road race. We spread out our rations of pretzels, sour balls, oranges and special mixture of water (80%) and Gatorade (20%)—not too sweet but with a little bit of kick. We loaded our goods in Ziploc bags and stuffed them in our pockets. We made one last visit

The Boston Athletic Association and the town of Hopkinton are well-prepared for the needs of competitors and spectators attending the 1996 race. Photo courtesy of FayFoto.

to the bathroom, thanked Tracy for her hospitality and jumped in Jeff's car for the short ride to the course. When he had taken us as far as he could, we disembarked and thanked him profusely.

At that time, we were faced with the reality of finding a way to get into the race. The subject had been discussed over and over by the four of us for months. It was my intention to work my way down the route and jump in after the start. But luckily Richie talked me into experiencing the thrill of crossing the starting line. So we maneuvered past policeman, race officials and National Guardsmen with our chests covered, feeling like members of the French underground stealing past German Soldiers.

We searched for other bandits, examining other competitors' sneakers to see if they had a computer micro-chip tied to their shoelaces. This chip was used to read the time of the numbered runners via satellite. A runner without a chip was one of us. So with opinions bountiful and answers scarce, we decided to sit on the sidewalk of a side street and wait. Just one hour to go.

When we had been watching television earlier that morning, we tuned in WCVB TV, Channel 5 in Boston. Mike Lynch, the head sportscaster, introduced Marty Liquori, the race analyst. At that moment, Liquori took advantage of his air time to castigate the dreaded bandits. His tirade included, "You've had ninety-nine years to qualify. If you haven't done it by now, then stay home!"

I was outraged. Who was he to tell me that I didn't deserve the opportunity to run in this race. I had been forced to undergo corrective heart surgery before I could even train for the race. I had to receive a cortisone shot for my left knee and had struggled through months of physical therapy. I had trained through the worst winter in the history of Boston. I had run in fifteen inches of snow. I had run in 8° weather. I had to arrange baby sitters for my son in order to train—all in order to fulfill a childhood dream.

Why was some person who didn't qualify for the race but had a political connection, or was part of some foreign tour group, or had sufficient funds to make a large contribution to a charity, or just happened to have his/ her name pulled out of a hat, more welcome than I was? This was as much my race as theirs. For thirty years, I have stood with my family in Newton being chased by cheek-pinching aunts, or in Cleveland Circle with inebriated college friends, or at the twenty-mile mark with my wife and newborn son. How many races did Marty Liquori stand in the rain or beating sun to cheer a ten-minute miler who simply dared to try? Listen Marty—you are our guest. So mind your manners, pick up your check, watch the race and thank you for my additional motivation—because when I cross that finish line some twenty-six miles down the road, with not a number but instead with the weathered history of the Boston Marathon tradition in my blood—I will consider myself qualified!

Shuttle buses from all over the state continue to move in and out while BAA officials continue to bite their fingernails. Dave McGillivray, the race's technical director, starts to connect with officials and police chiefs in each town along the route. Soon he will hear voices from each town on his two-way radio and he prays that they will give him the "all clear."

But until those connections are made, the carnival in Hopkinton continues. The Hopkinton First Congregational Church is across the street from the starting line. On this day, the powers in charge take advantage of this special event to greatly increase the size of the usual assembly. As the runners prepare for their run, they can be bombarded by renditions of "Amazing Grace" and signs such as "At Heartbreak Hill, You Can Do It Through Jesus Christ Who Gives You Strength."

Runners spend the last minutes before the race in one of two ways—either they are filled with nervous banter or they slip into their own cocoon. John "Younger" Kelley used to focus on any thought that didn't involve the race. "It was important to put the race in perspective. If you didn't, you would go crazy. I remember trying to focus on the fields and treed woods of Hopkinton while at the same time ignoring all the talk around me. I often thought that my friends and peers must have thought I was jerk, but that's just the way I was on race day."

Olympic silver medalist John Treacy likes to spend the minutes before the race talking and being sociable. "There is no animosity between the competitors because we all understand the mortality of a marathon. There is no reason to get the competitive juices flowing at this point. The twenty-mile mark is where you evaluate and assess your competition."

1976 winner Jack Fultz also likes to talk with other runners before the race. "It's important to have 'relaxed concentration.' It's not like being a sprinter who needs to be hyper-focused. A marathoner who is obsessed with concentration will not be able to relax sufficiently enough to run to his or her potential."

At this point, the runners have made peace with the Lord, or Yahweh, or Mohammed, or the Golden Sneaker god. Now it is out of the hands of the runner and in the hands of the weatherman and Father Time. Passing minutes are slowly displayed on the runners' digital watches in much the same way that they were ticked off the time pieces of derby-donned gentlemen of years gone by. Stretching, searching for the most inconspicuous pine tree, and babbling nervously seem to move the clock until the officials begin to organize the start of the wheelchair competition at 11:45.

Upon the call for the runners, competitors make their way to the starting line which is guarded on one side by the Dough Boy Statue of a World War I infantry soldier with gun on his shoulder and a concerned look on his bronzed face. Some note the ominous fact that the statue of the Dough Boy has stood over this start for decades, yet he continues to march in the opposite direction of the race.

With the soldier acting as guard on one side, the other side is even more threatening—a cemetery. This resting place causes some runners to contemplate their mere mortality.

Prior to the start of the race, the elite runners find refuge in a church fifty yards from the starting line. At 11:45, they are marched through the neighboring cemetery in order to gain unharrassed access to the starting line. This strange change in scenery always created a wide range of emotions for Uta Pippig. "One moment I'm sitting in a church where you are supposed to be quiet and respectful. Before you know it, you're walking through a cemetery around graves and by tombstones. In a different way, I feel a quiet connection with the people who might lay beneath my feet. Then, after quickly reflecting upon the lives of people who are no longer with us, I walk out on the street and there stand thousands of people who are waiting to start the most alive competition in the world. In the span of five minutes, I have passed through every facet of life."

1996. **Os and Bev Oskam of Vancouver, Canada were married at the Hopkinton First Congregational Church at eight in the morning. The bride wore a customized gown for running while the groom looked equally dapper in his tux and sneakers.**

❧ ❧ ❧ ❧ ❧

1984. **Tom Fleming, one of the contenders for this year's championship, was unhappy with the press that Englishman Geoff Smith received. "I just don't think Geoff Smith is as great as he thinks he is. I know this marathon too well. Geoff Smith went out at New York (Marathon) fast, he then tired, fell down and was lying on the finish line like a dead dog." So much for no animosity between the runners before the race. Geoff Smith went on to win the race.**

1995. **Cosmas Ndeti was upset to read that *USA Today* reported he wasn't capable of winning this year's race. So at the pre-race press conference, Cosmas made a brief statement: "I will give my interview on the course." He carried the *USA Today* story to the starting line with him and went on to win his third Boston Marathon.**

Os and Bev Oskam were married prior to the running of the 100th Boston Marathon.
Photo courtesy of FayFoto.

The band baptizes the largest one day sporting event, in the world, with a Rockwellian version of the National Anthem. With the sound of the "Star Spangled Banner" reverberating through the air, race officials begin to hyperventilate while the runners contemplate their mission and try to control their emotions. Over the last year, these competitors have logged thousands of miles in an effort to reach their respective goals. Whether that goal is winning, breaking a time barrier or simply finishing, each benchmark is of equal importance and is the source of serious thought in these last seconds before the gun.

"Everyone who finishes the Boston Marathon will have their own great moment in sports. Each one of us, on this day, can achieve greatness." —Dr. Sheehan

All of those long runs made in the dark of the night, on the wet slippery streets of a New England winter day, on a monotonous treadmill in Oslo, Norway, or during a pre-work run through the streets of Tokyo, or on a quick five-mile run squeezed in on a lunch hour—all of these commitments lead to this one moment. All the pain that has been endured—the sore knees, the blisters on the feet, the dog bites, the games of chicken with some pick-up truck with Yodel wrappers on the dash board, all those nightmares of forgetting your sneakers.

Kathy Switzer, one of the pioneer women runners, lived through a real life running nightmare in 1976. With the running craze in full swing, traffic into the starting line was at a standstill. Switzer, stuck on some side street, was forced to draw her number with a magic marker on the back of a newspaper, and jump from the car. She raced to the starting line, to find that no one was there. Around the corner, she heard some noise. She remembered the starting line was moved so she sprinted up and around the Hopkinton Common. There, she jumped across the starting line, was greeted by Will Cloney and the gun went off one minute later.

Two-time champion and Olympic gold medal winner Joan Benoit confessed that she had a nightmare just before the 1983 race. In her dream, she was window-shopping in some of Hopkinton boutiques when the gun was sounded. She quickly ran out of the shops and had to join the race in the back of the pack. She was relieved when she woke up.

MPC: Throughout the months leading up to the Marathon, I had experienced several dreams about the race. Some visions had me running jubilantly the last yards of the race while other dreams had me missing the start for whatever reason. Needless to say, my subconscious was quite aware of the magnitude of this event and the significance that it played in my life.

The course ahead will provide many mental and physical peaks and valleys. But now is not the time to analyze whether or not you trained properly, or if you ate too much pasta the night before, or if you should have gone to the bathroom again. There is no turning back now. Your year of commitment is about to face the test. The

1982. Alberto Salazar's bravado showed a slight crack when he admitted, "Standing on the starting line, we are all cowards."

❧ ❧ ❧ ❧ ❧

1983. Winner Greg Meyer stood on the starting line with feelings of fear and anxiety. "With the course starting on a narrow street (49' 10"—21 bodies can fit) and moving downhill, all of your training could be for naught with one trip over someone's feet. I wish I could fall asleep and wake up somewhere in Natick."

❧ ❧ ❧ ❧ ❧

1990. Seven-time champion Jean Driscoll confessed that she felt that she didn't belong on the starting line. She proved herself wrong by winning her first Boston Marathon that year. If a champion of that caliber questions herself, just imagine the doubts that creep into the psyche of the average three-hour marathoner.

(*Left to right*) Michael Radley, Rich Twombly, Jack Radley and the author are ready and rearing to go as they pose on the morning of the race. Photo courtesy of Barbara Mulligan.

trials and tribulations were endured in order to stand on this line, and have the opportunity to conquer the next twenty-six plus miles. Truth is just a few ticks of the clock away.

The adrenaline is flowing, the helicopters are flying, and the music from the bandstand is playing. It all seems surreal, like a scene right out of the movie *Apocalypse Now.*

MPC: From the moment that I decided to run the Boston Marathon, I was in complete denial. Running non-stop for twenty-six plus miles is an idea which in general, is unhealthy if not asinine. Sure, I've always had wild and exciting ideas, but acting on them was a different matter altogether.

As the months of the calendar began to flip towards the spring, I buried the fear of failure deep into my subconscious. In reality, I had no right to be standing on the starting line. But there I stood, with no parachute, while the starter cocked the gun. My chances for escaping were gone, and the fear of failure was starting to flow from the subconscious to the conscious. I was starting to realize that I had swum out too far and now I was caught in a Nantucket riptide. Who was I kidding? Maybe Marty Liquori was right. Maybe I should have stayed home. Maybe dreams and reality are set in different conscious states for a reason. Maybe, just maybe, this time I had bitten off more than I could chew. But the tide was taking me and I let it.

There is no question that the possibility of failure holds great danger for each individual's ego. But at the same time the possibility of achieving one's goal can bring great fulfillment.

With just minutes to the start, Frances Scott Key's last note is played, the numbered athletes are in place, the bandit runners are filtering to the back, the helicopters are hovering overhead and the starter's arm is raised. . . .

PART II

A RACE FOR THE AGES

Runners set their watches and prepare to take their first steps toward Boston in 1994.
Photo courtesy of Victah Sailer.

MILE ONE

One by one the runners fall into place as they await the sound of the gun. Courteous hellos are now replaced with stern faces and extended elbows. Anxious runners, in the middle of the pack, are starting to gasp for air while the elite runners in the front seem to be frozen in time.

MPC: In the shadows on Grove Street, a half-mile away from the starting line, stood Richie, Rad, our newfound friend Michael, myself and some five thousand other outlaws lurking in the shadows on Grove Street (Jack Radley had procured himself a spot up ahead with the lottery runners). Although the atmosphere was festive, there was at the same time a mood of uncertainty. Standing between the bandits and the numbered runners was a line of bike racks and ten of the biggest National Guardsmen that the state could muster. Over the loudspeaker system, which was set up along the street, a disc jockey told jokes, yelled out the runners' names, had the runners do the wave and played music from the Steve Miller Band ("I want to fly like an eagle to the sea, fly like an eagle let my spirit carry me ...") in an effort to keep the crowd settled and occupied. As the hour drew closer to noon, my adrenaline level rose dramatically—first the helicopters from the media networks covering the race, then the Star Spangled Banner and at last the sound of the gun.

The firing of the gun, though, meant more waiting, increasing anxiety in the back of the pack, which was estimated would take over an hour to reach the starting line. This was bad news for Rad, Richie, Michael and me—there we were in the front row against the bike racks which was the equivalent of being stuck against the stage during a Rolling Stones concert.

Grove Street which feeds into Main Street seemed to have some movement around 12:15. Then the National Guardsmen moved the bike racks and allowed the bandits into the race. Commendably, the BAA had decided to continue the tradition of an "open" race and avert a riot by 5,000 committed athletes.

The joy of joining the celebration of the 100th Boston Marathon brought a euphoric reaction from the merry bandits. As we broke into a slow jog, there were hugs, high fives and shouts of ecstasy. People showered the above trees with sweatshirts, pants and gloves as we worked our way towards the promised land.

There is a unique bond among runners. Like friendships formed during wars, these momentary, but memorable acquaintances are formed through a sharing of fears, hopes and desires. During those vulnerable moments, as we wait to enter the arena, instant friendships are formed with the exchange of a word or a smile.

Finally the moment is here. The starter, who has been a member of the Brown family of Hopkinton since the early 1900s, raises his ancient colonial pistol and fires the weapon, thus christening the race and sending the runners down Route 135 towards Boston. What the competitors hear is a pre-recorded howitzer. The gun is connected by cable to clocks throughout the route.

MPC: Then we were off. As we turned into Main Street and approached the starting line we realized what the Marathon was all about—it was like a personal surprise party for each and every runner. Standing on roofs, perched on tree limbs, leaning through windows, from decks, porches and car tops was a blur of people screaming encouragement to the runners. It was as though we were heroes coming home from war.

Looking down Route 135 towards Boston, the runners can only see a short length of the course because of the sharp turn at the bottom of the first hill. Runners and wheelchair competitors must control themselves in order to proceed smartly and safely. A disorderly start can result in injury or even death. Runners must be careful

1996. Because of the magnitude of the field, the BAA has organized corrals to separate the runners. The elite runners were in the front of the pack on Main Street; qualifying runners were stationed on Hayden Rowe which lies perpendicular to Main Street along the the town green; parallel to Hayden Rowe lies Grove Street where the runners who have won a number in the lottery (5,000) or through charities, companies, running groups, or foreign tour groups (approximately 6,000), or those who were part of the bandit brigade (approximately 5,000) stood anxious and ready. This collection of amateurs brought up the rear approximately a half mile from the starting line. All in all it took just over 30 minutes for approximately 45,000 runners to cross the starting line.

❧❧❧❧❧

1897. Tom Burke of the BAA didn't fire a gun to start the runners for the first race, but simply raised his hand at 12:19 and yelled, "GO!"

1900. Canadian John Barnard jumped the gun, causing the only restart in the race's history.

1915. Starter George Victory Brown, cattle fancier, shouted at the runners who were jockeying for position on the tight railroad bridge in Ashland, "Don't crowd here, you've got 26 miles ahead of you. Now kneel down and get ready."

1937. The original bandit runner, Peter Foley, a diamond cutter from Medford and later Winchester, is ordered to start five minutes behind the qualified runners. "Old Pete" was ruled ineligible because of his extreme age of eighty years. He finished the race.

1953. An unidentified runner showed up at the start with starting blocks. Officials convinced him that the blocks wouldn't make much of a difference in the outcome.

1966. Roberta Gibb, the first woman ever to run the Boston Marathon, hid behind a forsythia bush on the Hopkinton town green waiting for the gun to go off. As the runners moved over the starting line, she slipped into the pack. Women runners were not officially allowed to run the Boston Marathon until 1972.

1967. Will Cloney, Director of the BAA, placed his hand on the shoulder of competitor #261, checked the number on the runner's chest, and pushed the athlete back behind the snow fence with the other runners. In all the chaos before the race, Cloney didn't realize that he had just put his hand on Kathy Switzer, the first numbered woman ever to run the Marathon.

1977. Winner Jerome Drayton, of Canada, voiced his displeasure with the start of the race at the post-race press conference. He mocked the idea of having a starting point on a suburban street; complained that there was no countdown to the gun and that he was kicked, grabbed and almost pulled down when the gun was fired. He claims that he feared for his life.

and aware that a treacherous second half lies beyond the easy first half of the race.

1957 winner, John "Younger" Kelley, referring to the first half of the race: "It's a setup. It is so easy to be suckered in by this attractive course."

The starting point has been estimated at approximately 450 feet above sea level—the highest point on the course. In the first four miles, the course falls almost 300 feet. This circumstance has created much controversy considering that the race bottoms out at Kenmore Square (twenty-five mile mark) almost at sea level. This descent of 450 feet creates an illusion for both the non-runner and the Technical Committee of the Athlete Congress that the race is directly downhill; therefore in the eyes of the TAC, the Boston Marathon should not be regarded as a race of world class stature and regard.

In 1990, the TAC decided that the Boston Marathon, although steeped in tradition and history, could not and would not be a source of world or national records. Subsequently, the TAC reversed all world records set in Boston, and placed the ever-dreaded "Roger Maris Asterisk" next to the efforts and times of people like Joan Benoit Samuelson and Rob de Castella.

Guy Morse, the 1996 race director, feels that this decision is best handled by ignoring it:"Since the ruling, the best runners of the world have run Boston, and have been unable to break the world record which in itself is a testament to the toughness and validity of the Boston Course."

The disagreement continues between the TAC and the BAA, but the fact remains that the beginning of the course is steep and alluring. Therefore, competitors must keep close to their game plans no matter how good they feel early in the race. On the other hand, so-called game plans are a debatable issue.

Like all athletes, wheelchair competitors face challenges and obstacles in their efforts to meet their goal, as pictured here in the 1985 marathon. Photo courtesy of the *Boston Herald.*

Past winners Geoff Smith and Jim Knaub will tell you there is no such thing as a game plan. Both runners have a common strategy. Attack every inch of the course the same. Says Knaub, "Go for broke from the beginning to the end. If it's not your day, then it's not your day." Says Smith, "Line up and let's see who's best—whoever wins was the best that day."

The stretch of opening descents has proved to be treacherous over the years to both game plans and runners' health and underscores the need for concern and restraint. The hazard of the downhill start for the 1987 wheelchair competitors was compounded by roads that were slick with rain. The combination of inclement weather and the fact that these competitors routinely reach speeds of over 40 miles per hour in the first 100 yards, combined to cause an inevitable calamity.

  With the discharge of the starter's gun, 100 wheelchair runners pushed themselves off the starting line throwing a spray of water from each wheel. Jockeying for position, the runners quickly picked up speed when five-time winner Jim Knaub hit a rut in the street that caused him to tip. This provoked an inevitable chain reaction crash which left six competitors lying on the side of the road with a variety of injuries and damage to their racing chairs. The sight of wheelchair competitors crashing to the ground horrified the crowd who were largely unaware of the fact that well-

1968. Mrs. Howard Fish hid behind a telephone pole near the starting line. There she waited for her husband, Reverend Fish of Cambridge, to run by so she could join him. The minister and his wife were the first unofficial couple to ever run the Boston Marathon. Mrs. Fish beat her husband to the finish line.

1985. The start of the wheelchair competition in 1985 was a source of great controversy. Several competitors claimed that George Murray, the eventual winner, took off on the count of three instead of waiting for the starting gun. Murray denied this accusation. Murray was also accused of drafting off the press bus, an accusation he also denied. Frustrated opponents of Murray later obtained a notarized letter from both the motorcycle policeman and media members, who had been on the bus, confirming that Murray was told to pass the bus, but that he preferred to stay behind in an effort to avoid the blustery head winds of the day. Nothing came of this protest and Murray retained his championship.

conditioned disabled athletes face challenges and dangers just like any other athlete who accepts the challenge and strives to push beyond their personal limitations.

Jim Knaub was able to make adjustments to his chair and finish the race. Jim Baughan suffered a badly bruised forehead, but also finished the race, refusing medical help until he crossed the finish line. Two competitors were unable to continue because of damaged chairs.

Some track enthusiasts, such as Fred Lebow, the late Director of the New York Marathon, who was never a big supporter of the wheelchair competitors, took advantage of the accident to warn the people of Boston that they were, "flirting with disaster."

These warnings did not go unheeded—Boston bowed to these cries, and instituted a pace car in 1988 which governed the wheelchair athletes at a speed of 20 miles per hour for the length of the first descent. This controlled start takes ten seconds off the average competitor's time. Prize money for record times is accordingly pro-rated to take into account the ten-second differential.

Ten minutes later, race officials scramble to prepare for the start of the Men's and Women's Open at 12:00. At the front, stand the women and men's favorites. As they attempt to focus there is chaos all around them.

In keeping with the Marathon tradition, the starter fired the gun exactly at noon (this tradition has since been modified to provide for adjustments depending on potential situation). This year, at noon time, there was a problem. In front of the starting line stood a policeman and race official with a rope that was inexplicably tied to a tree. When the gun sounded, pre-race favorite Rob de Castella tripped over the rope. Fortunately, a race official cut the rope with a pocket knife, preventing further disaster.

Although de Castella donated some of the skin from his knees and elbows to the streets of Hopkinton, he jumped to his feet and was on his way. He was later quoted, "I either had to get up or be trampled by 10,000 runners." de Castella ended up finishing sixth in the race but handled the situation with grace. He claimed the fall was not a factor in the outcome.

Down the hill, the road curves sharply left, then back to the right, then right again as the runners make their way past the halfway mark. Here, they hit their first incline of the race. This small insignificant hill is actually one of the most critical sections of the race for the wheelchair competitors.

Jim Knaub has said, "there are only two hills on the course. The one in the first mile, and Citgo Hill [mile 25]. The Newton Hills are not as critical as these two. If you make it to the top side of the first hill before everyone else, you have a great chance of winning. It's like God picked you up and dropped you in the lead, and said it's your day."

If a wheelchair competitor loses contact with the lead pack on this hill, he or she will be incapable of drafting with the front-running group. This will force the athlete to make a move on their own. This effort to rejoin the leaders is unlikely to succeed considering the fact that the lead group is working as a cohesive unit which is moving faster while at the same time utilizing less energy. Separation from the pack at the first hill can add as much as ten minutes to the wheelchair competitor's overall time because of the inability to draft. The loss of time and energy eliminates the trailing wheelchair runner from championship contention.

For the elite runners in the open field, the first mile can also be a nuisance, but for other reasons. Bill Rodgers, the four-time winner, doesn't particularly like the start. "The descent at the outset gives runners, who aren't necessarily world class, the opportunity to stay with the

1996. Prior to the race, bandits were discouraged from running because of the large group of numbered runners. Some bandits placed ads in the local newspaper offering upwards of $1,000 for a number from qualified runners who had a number but couldn't run. Other bandits ran the route the day before and still others rallied through the Internet agreeing to meet at the starting line at 8:00 A.M. to begin the race.

❧ ❧ ❧ ❧ ❧

1981. Craig Virgin, the second place finisher, recommended, "Don't do anything crazy in the first ten miles."

❧ ❧ ❧ ❧ ❧

1936. Jimmy "Cigar" Connors was famous for his crazy outfits, smoking cigars and driving race director Jock Semple crazy. In 1935, he ran the opening miles while smoking two cigars at the same time. In 1932, while running the race he jumped on the running board of a car and rejoined the runners at the twenty-five mile mark and finished the race. In 1937, Connors crossed the finish line wearing pink pants, a yellow beret and smoking the inevitable cigar.

Bridge at Ashland
Start of Marathon, year, ?

Just minutes before the 1906 start, runners pose for a picture at the starting line on the High Street Railroad Bridge in Ashland. Photo courtesy of the Boston Athletic Assocation.

leaders long enough to be bothersome." Rodgers observed that on a level course, the world class runners would leave impostors in the dust, referring to the camera hound or cigar-smoking runner who is more interested in being photographed than in finishing the race.

In the meat of the pack, runners are still jockeying for position by jumping up on sidewalks and around parked cars in an effort to pass slow starters and get off to a quicker start. At the back of the pack, runners are moving like rush hour traffic on the Expressway in Boston—barely.

Up the hill and to the left, in the last quarter of the mile, the runners pass a nursery. Just beyond the nursery, sits a barn from old Tebeau's Farm. Back in the 20s, 30s and 40s runners gathered at this spot to change and undergo their pre-race physicals. Mary Tebeau, an Ashland school teacher, eventually sold the land to the Mezitt family.

The Mezitts, who, with over 900 acres, are the largest landowners in the town of Hopkinton, still work the land under the name of Weston Nurseries. They grow everything from a special Rhodendron, which blooms for the race, to Christmas trees. Brothers Wayne and Roger Mezitt remember when the race started on their farm at a spot called "Lucky Rock." The rock was dubbed lucky because of a streak of quartz that ran through the middle of the ledge.

After getting dressed in the old barn, the runners were herded by the chief shepherd, race director Jock Semple, behind a snow fence (bull pen) until one of the Browns fired his gun.

Runners from the middle and back of the pack are just starting to break into a jog after crossing the starting line in 1991. Photo courtesy of the *Boston Herald*.

Although the Mezitts have fond memories of this day, their business suffers badly throughout the holiday because of the tight traffic control which is maintained throughout the race.

As the runners race to the top of this hill, they pass a field called Mahar's Meadow. At this spot the competitors have completed the first chapter of this twenty-six mile journey.

Hopefully the runners at the back are approaching the starting line.

MPC: It took just 28 minutes for the 37,500 numbered runners to cross the starting line. After crossing the starting line, the route moved down hill past tailgate parties, (one had a stereo perpetually playing the theme from the movie "Rocky") and woods filled with runners relieving themselves. The running was slow and circuitous as the crowd of runners found its pace. This was a pattern which would be prevalent throughout the race. As Rad, Richie, Michael and I passed the one-mile mark, we checked our watches to find out that the first mile took us 13 minutes. The lead pack ran the initial mile in 4:33.

Geoff Smith (left) and friend play the role of queen bees while being closely followed by interested suitors.
Photo courtesy of Jeff Johnson.

MILE TWO

Early in the race, the athletes move as a collective mass of humanity. Spectators waiting for the runners to come around the corner can hear the oncoming stampede. As the athletes come into sight, the wheelchair competitors and the elite runners move swiftly by, like queen bees, being chased by a swarm of healthy worker bees.

As the following pack of runners continues to be herded forward, it is impossible to identify individual competitors. The majority of the runners have been unable to open up to a comfortable pace. Each step must be carefully placed in order to prevent stepping on another runner's foot.

The spectators along the early stretch come primarily from surrounding homes. Any outsider interested in seeing the race from this vantage point would have had to arrive before 6:30 when the streets are closed to vehicular traffic.

The neighborhood is mostly rural. Incorporated in 1715, the town stretches 28.17 miles long. It was named after Edward Hopkins, the Governor of Connecticut in the 1640s, whose monetary donation to Harvard University was in turn invested in land. This land, which was inhabited by the Quansigomog Indians, later became known as Hopkinton. Over the last century, the town's identity had been formed through its association with the race. At times, the race had been a great source of community argument, but in general the town has welcomed the runners with open arms and open bathroom doors.

As the runners complete mile one and crest the first hill, the course then takes a mild dip, and shuffles left for about a quarter of a mile. Within this segment of the race, the runners are delightfully entertained by the Vermont Fiddlers—compliments of Art Fairbanks, the owner of Art's Auto Body.

Fifteen years ago, Art shut down the shop, which sits on the right side of the course about 1.2 miles from the starting line, and decided to give the Vermont Fiddlers a stage for their biggest concert of the year.

In the early days, the entire field of runners could race by Art's garage in five minutes. When they passed, Art would take advantage of the festivities to stop re-aligning cars, in order to admire the men and women who were passing by his stop. As there is no business to be done on Marathon Day, Art figured, "if you can't beat 'em—join 'em."

The runners make a great audience as they dance, jig and check to see if they're in Galway, Ireland or Hopkinton, Massachusetts.

The mile continues, with a wave of quick-hitting ups and downs. An occasional house can be glimpsed amongst the woods and fields on each side of the road. Halfway through the mile, the runners pass Clinton Street and its admiring residents.

Right before the two mile mark sits the Ashland/Hopkinton border where the baton is handed from one town to the next. At the border is a friendly local tavern called TJ's. The owner, John Tomasz, looks forward to Marathon weekend all year, and it usually doesn't disappoint. From Friday through Monday, the place is hopping. On Sunday night, TJ's offers a basic pasta dinner for runners who have found lodging near the starting line. For five dollars, its all that you can eat. For Monday, the tavern applies for and receives (contrary to the police chief's protests) a permit to party-hardy outside. With a disc-jockey spinning tunes and a cook flipping burgers on the barbecue, its a good time for all.

After TJ's the road is flat and residential, leading you to mile three.

MPC: The road continued to be crowded and festive.

1990. **Runner David Cantone had pushed himself in his training to prepare for the Marathon. In order to make it all worthwhile, David needed to cross the finish line in Boston.**

Along with the thousands of other runners, David made his way through the first mile and began his assault on the second mile of the race. The mob of runners was beginning to spread out when David noticed something on the side of the road. He did a double take and quickly darted to the aid of the man with his eyes rolled back into his head who was spitting up blood.

Running the Marathon was now a far second on Cantone's list of priorities. He immediately summoned nearby Red Cross volunteers and together they got the patient, who was suffering a Grand Mal seizure, to the nearest hospital. The stricken runner was attended to and released later that afternoon. David Cantone, who had sat with his new friend throughout the day, hailed a cab so that the two of them could get back to Boston.

Sometimes things don't work out exactly as planned. In the case of David Cantone, he set out to run a marathon and instead he will be remembered as the Good Samaritan. As the cab rambled over the finish line 24 miles later, the world was just a little better.

Above: An aerial view of the early stages of the 1935 race. Photo courtesy of the Boston Public Library Print Dept.
Below: Runners in the 1996 Marathon move to the side of the road to slap hands
with the fans. Photo courtesy of Jacob Morey.

By this point, breathing became more settled after the initial excitement of the start and first mile. Runners hugged the sides of the road in order to high five the fans who were extending their hands.

Kids along the side of the road were being baptized in the waters of the Boston Marathon. Parents brought their young ones to the route in order to expose them to "the tradition." When you live in these parts, the Boston Marathon is a part of being

As Richie, Rad and I ran by the crowd, with our mustard-colored shirts with BOB (Boston's Official Bandit) on the front, the crowd would cheer—"Go Bob, Bob and Bob!" or "What about Bob?" An elementary school teacher of mine once told me that the nicest sound anyone could hear was their name. For four and a half hours, I was the happiest Michael ever to hear the sweet word "BOB."

Halfway through the second mile, a sign on the left side of the road summed up the coming journey—"Dead Men Walking."

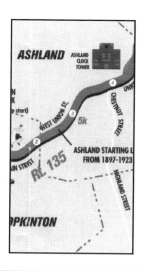

MILE THREE

The first two-tenths of Mile Three is a level run through a residential neighborhood. In the third tenth of the mile, the road moves straight, but begins to ascend.

Early in the third mile, the runners move past a water stop at Prosperous Gardens, a local nursery. Owner Dick Preservagi looks forward to this day as a spectator, but hates the day as a business owner. I asked him for his impression of the race, the runners and the event in general. He remained silent for ten seconds, as though he was searching for his handy thesaurus, and finally exulted, "I don't know what it is, but when the mass of humanity passes by . . . I-I-I just love it."

The road inclines to the right before it slopes off to the left. At the half-mile mark, the runners pass the local Knights of Columbus and the Ashland State Park. From there, the mile moves downhill.

Uta Pippig—"In the first five miles, it's important to run your race. The early downhills make it essential to slow yourself and stay at your pace. At the same time, on a nice spring day, I like to take the opportunity to appreciate the new green leaves on the many trees in Hopkinton and Ashland."

At approximately the 2.7 mile mark, the runners move past the site of Steven's Corner which was the location of the start of the race from 1899 to 1924. It is just down the road from the spot where Holton and Graham had ridden their bikes and declared the starting point of the race. A quarter of a century later the start was moved back to Hopkinton.

Ashland was never truly recognized for its contribution to the race until recent times. The town of Ashland was better known for manufacturing clocks and watches thanks to local inventor Henry Warren. Warren designed and created the first self-winding clock during the Depression, and people moved to the town in order to find work in the prospering clock factory. General Electric eventually joined Warren as a 49% partners in the project which proved to be a wise investment.

The Ashland High School adopted its nickname by the trade which helped the town prosper—the Clock-Towners. The town itself was actually named after a rich country estate. A town incorporator and admirer of Senator Henry Clay adopted the name of Ashland from one of Clay's three properties in the state of Kentucky. The town was known as Unionville until 1846 when it incorporated after acquiring land from the three surrounding towns, including Hopkinton.

The course levels off at the three-mile mark, just past the entrance to Ashland High School on your left.

Traffic and spectators along the route have always been a risk to the competitors and each other. Halfway through the third mile, Leo Girard, of Brockton, Massachusetts was run over by a motorcycle. After receiving medical care for badly cut knees, elbows and shoulder, he jumped back in the race and climbed into ninth position before falling back and finishing fifteenth.

MPC: The third mile helped acclimate us to the style and pace of the race. After a couple of miles, we quickly realized that one of the keys to this day would be patience.

Our pace had quickened to nine-minute miles, but that was accomplished with the difficult navigation of walkers and slower runners.

We also figured out that going to the first tables at the water stops could be hazardous to our health. Instead, we zeroed in on the end tables, which allowed us the opportunity to move in and out of the pit stop safely and quickly.

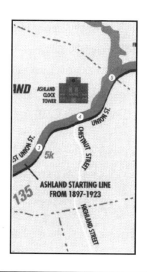

MILE FOUR

At this juncture of the race, the surrounding area begins to become more commercial. The road continues on a downward grade moving left before straightening itself and going right. At the 3.1 mile mark, there is a small shopping plaza on the left which is occupied by your basic video store and insurance agency. On your right, you can smell the grease burning at the Honey Dew donut shop while watching the kids lick ice creams from a neighboring Tasty Treat. In the middle of the road sits a dangerous cement island that is better known to the fans and athletes of the race as "Three Mile Island." This cement protrusion stretches for about 20 yards. Wheelchair competitors need to be especially careful coming around the bend. Their speeds could be in excess of 25 miles per hour coming down the long downgrade approaching the islands. Although the island is well-marked with cones and police tape, these hazards can jump on you in hurry—especially if your head is down or you're drafting or following another competitor too closely. This is one of the spots in the race where being unfamiliar with the course can be a detriment.

At 3.3 miles, you continue past a drug store and a pizza shop. The course, at this point, turns uphill and to the right. On the sidewalks, the number of spectators have increased.

MPC: Halfway through the fourth mile, my sisters, Maureen and Cathy, were waiting with a sign and their guarded optimism. I had informed my family before the race that no matter how bad I looked they must lie and tell me that I'm doing great. I knew that my margin of error would be slim so there was no room on the course for any doubt or negative thought.

Each time I came upon a family member or friend, I realized that I was loved. Although this seems insignificant to the capacity of a runner to run a race, the further the runner moves down the course, the more he or she will understand that this event is physical, mental and emotional.

Wheelchair competitors carefully navigate the treacherous Three Mile Island in Ashland during the 100th running of the Boston Marathon. Photo courtesy of FayFoto.

A quarter of mile up the road we had planned on waving to a distant acquaintance. I couldn't believe our disappointment when he wasn't there. You would have thought we had been left at the altar.

As Mile Four turns flat and straight, the course moves through a small residential section before passing an old burial ground, and then a school on the left. At the next set of lights at the Main Street intersection, runners pass the spot where the old hotels, the Central House and the Columbia House, were located. In the early 1900s, runners ate their pre-race dinner and underwent physicals there.

With nine-tenths of the mile finished, the runners pass the Ashland Clock Tower perched on the roof of the Ashland Technology Building. At the top of the structure, a giant clock faces kitty-corner toward the race. In the old days, Clarence DeMar used the giant timepiece to check his pace early in the race.

Clarence DeMar, content with being known as a humble printshop worker, is probably the most unknown superstar in Boston sports history. Winning his first Boston Marathon in 1911 and his seventh in 1930, DeMar was truly one of the greatest American athletes of all time.

DeMar could have possibly won ten or more marathons, but a local doctor had warned DeMar that he had an irregular heart beat which could be fatal. Even stairclimbing should be avoided, never mind a marathon. So DeMar skipped ten of the next eleven years, in accordance with the doctor's orders.

DeMar eventually got tired of running back and forth to work as his main source of exercise, so he entered the race in 1922 and won the first of five in that decade. When once asked the name of the doctor who diagnosed his cardiac condition, he answered, "I won't tell you his name but he recently died of a heart attack. He must have been listening to his own heart."

Clarence resided in Melrose, Massachusetts where he taught Sunday School and was a boy scout leader. He was a World War I Veteran and a 1915 graduate of Harvard with an Associates degree in art and a Master's degree from Boston University.

Although DeMar was quiet and reserved off the course, he became a fierce competitor once the gun was fired. He felt that the Boston Marathon belonged to him, and acted that way. Two fans can attest to his intensity by being recipients of right crosses from the championship runner. One of the fans had asked for an autograph in the middle of the race, and the other had poured ice water on the back of his legs.

DeMar's life was running. He once said, "I would be happy if I died while running." DeMar would get his wish. Late in life he was hospitalized with intestinal cancer. His doctor was mortified to find the great runner jogging in place in his hospital room. Although the doctor pleaded with Clarence to rest, DeMar continued on and hours later died a fulfilled man.

Clarence was certainly DeMar(velous).

As the runners pass the same clock that DeMar had, almost a century ago, they hardly glance at the old dinosaur because they have digital watches and a number of clocks on the side of the road to remind them that they should have trained harder.

Above: The incomparable Clarence DeMar runs toward one of his seven championships.
Below: Victor MacAuley, Clarence DeMar and Chuck Mellor (L to R) run stride for
stride in 1925. Photos courtesy of the *Boston Herald.*

1997. With the hopes of his small village in Mexico riding on his proud shoulders, German Silva found out firsthand about the dangers of the Three Mile Island. As members of the Kenyan running group in front of him left a water stop, they failed to negotiate the island, sending Kenyan Charles Tangus to the ground. The following Silva gave his best shot at the high hurdles but was tripped up. With damaged legs, he picked himself up to finish a sad fourth.

1976. Because there were no clocks provided for the runners so that they could calculate splits, Jack Fultz decided to use his placement in the race as his timer. He knew, if he was running in the top ten, then he was running at speed which was consistent with what he needed in order to run a good race.

1923. The Red Cross held a Red Tag sale in Ashland before the running of the Marathon. Proceeds were used to purchase first aid kits for the local schools.

1989. The area in front of the Cherry Blossom was the site of a near tragedy. As a pack of runners was making its way past the gathered spectators, a deranged runner reached into the crowd and grabbed a little girl. As he dragged her down the street, the other spectators followed in pursuit. The crazed wanna-be kidnapper released the girl and jumped in the nearby pond in an attempt to foil the chase by the mob and now the police. He was quickly reeled in from his impromptu biathlon with cries of "I'm Jesus Christ," which made it unnecessary to test him for narcotics.

Diagonally across from the clock, on the right side before the intersection, is an empty lot which is utilized on Marathon Day by the local chapter of the Lions Club for its annual Flea Market. This is their best fundraiser of the year, sending people home with smiles and junk that they don't really need. You wonder if some of that stuff is as old as the race.

Past the street on the same side is a Dairy Queen ice cream stand. This is one of those spots where you see a complete nutritional polarization between the runners and the season ticketholders of Dairy Queen although on hot days the franchise has been known to get an occasional athlete at their "run-thru."

As the end of mile approaches, you are sandwiched by two businesses. On the right is Cherry Blossom, a Chinese food restaurant. Each year the restaurant sets up tables of water in front to provide the runners with refreshment. The restaurant doesn't do much business during the day and actually loses money by staying open, but they hope their gesture of hospitality creates some community goodwill.

On the left side of the Four Mile mark sandwich is Tom's Autobody which is beautifully situated above the course. It does not resemble your average auto body shop, and its owner, Tom McClements, likes to recount a whimsical history of the lot.

In the late eighteen hundreds, the Perini family, who are known in these parts for owning the Boston Braves and Perini Construction, owned an estate on this site. It was the envy of the town. The mansion sported a fish pond in the shape of a fish, cathedral windows and the old man's favorite toy—a baby grand piano. During the spring and summer days, Perini enjoyed sitting up on the hill and, with the windows open, treating the town with a piano concerto.

Along with the many other amenities, the Perini

estate was the first house in the town to have electricity, a blessing that proved to be the source of tragedy when a northeastern storm blew into town. The blizzard, which was accompanied with blustery winds, knocked down the electric wires exposing them to the wet storm. This ignited a fire at the Perini mansion and burned the estate to the ground. As the old man sadly reviewed the damage, he was overjoyed to find that his pride and joy—the baby grand piano—had been saved to play another day.

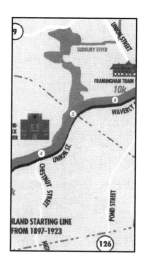

MILE FIVE

After the Four Mile mark, the runners are greeted by refreshing Bracketts Pond on the left side of the course. In the middle of the road runners must be aware of another set of cement islands. The road then forks left before passing Beckongreen LTD, a nursery, on the left. Here the names of friends and associates who are running the race are listed on an outside board normally used to advertise flower sales. Many sweatshirts and coats are thrown into the nursery's parking lot by runners who are beginning to overheat.

The course continues to snake uphill, left and right, moving past DRC Auto Service garage and the Sri Lakshemi Temple at the Framingham/Ashland border.

The Sri Lakshemi Temple is a Mecca for Hindus living in northeast America. Worshippers come from as far as New Jersey to shed their shoes and pay homage. On the Temple's magnificent tower, which rises 50 feet into the sky, is a statue of Lakshemi, the goddess of Wealth. Standing at her sides are the dwarapalika—the female gatekeepers. On Marathon day, the runners will call upon whatever god or goddess who will help them move down the road.

Mile Five is a mixture of residential, commercial and undeveloped land. It is not a mile of great impact in the grand scheme of the Boston Marathon. In fact, some runners are completely indifferent through this stretch and must bear down in order to stay focused.

Somewhere in Mile Five, the 1967 Boston Marathon was changed forever. It was a time when most of the country was in the midst of some form of change or protest and the Marathon was not exempt to the challenges of the oppressed.

51

It was in this year that Kathy Switzer attempted to run and unintentionally became the first numbered woman ever to run the Boston Marathon. As far as she was concerned, she was an athlete in pursuit of a goal—not a rebel or troublemaker. "It didn't say 'Men Only' on the application" she said later.

With her head covered by the hood of her sweatshirt at the starting line, she took her spot shoulder-to-shoulder with the other competitors. The gun was fired and the numbered runners trotted their way through Hopkinton and into Ashland. Little by little, the word began to spread that there was a woman running with a number. The word reached to the press bus where race officials Jock Semple and Will Cloney were speeding their way towards the renegade.

At the time, Switzer's only concern was one of vanity. "I couldn't wait to take off my old gray sweat-suit and show off my beautiful running suit that I had on underneath. I wanted to prove that a woman athlete didn't need to be masculine or a tomboy, but can be feminine and an athlete."

The flatbed truck with the photographers moved past Ms. Switzer before she could discard her sweats so she decided to leave them on. The press bus then passed, and pulled over to the side as Cloney and Semple jumped off. The infuriated officials were determined to remove the official number which sat mockingly on the front of that genderless sweat-top.

But, if the dynamic defenders of male separatism were to get to their adversary, then they would have to make their way past Switzer's muscle-bound boyfriend, Tom Miller who was running side-by-side with his girlfriend. As Semple got to her ("Cloney tried to catch her first, but he was too bloody slow"), he yelled for this marathon alien to "get out of my race!" He then reached for Switzer and began to pull off the number 261. Instinctively, Tom Miller, who proved chivalry was far from

1976. With the thermometer topping the 100º degree mark, fluids became a matter of necessity. As Jack Fultz ran towards the Framingham border in Mile Five, he noticed a makeshift shower on the side of the road. Someone had strapped a hose to the top of a step ladder and turned the water on. Fultz decided to deviate off the course and enjoy this respite from the baking sun. As Fultz stood under the water for five or six seconds, he convinced himself that he was making an "investment in time." He went on to win the race.

1983. At the five-mile checkpoint Ethiopian runner, Abraha Gebrehiwet Aregha was the early leader. Along with his running form, his musical tastes were being critiqued by Marty Liquori. Abraha was wearing a Sony Walkman set as he trotted down Route 135. Liquori told his audience to ignore the leader because, in Liquori's eyes, anyone who would wear a musical device while running in a world class race shouldn't be taken seriously.

Abraha eventually fell from the lead after seven miles and finished without his Walkman. It was later learned that the music lover had actually been doing a live commercial for Sony. He finished 110th with a time of 2:21:57.

In later years, fellow marathoners grew to respect Aregha as a formidable runner. Aregha has a sub 2:12 marathon on his resume.

Jock Semple feels the wrath of Kathy Switzer's running companion, Tom Miller, in the 1967 Boston Marathon as Semple attempts to rip Kathy's number from her jersey. Women were not allowed to "officially" run the Boston Marathon until 1972. Photo courtesy of the Boston Public Library.

In an effort to look both athletic and feminine, Kathy Switzer runs the first four miles in a lovely black-and-white ensemble. Photo courtesy of the Boston Public Library Print Dept.

1968. *The Boston Globe* reported that Jock Semple was in charge of keeping "babes" off the course. He was later quoted, "They will run over my dead body!"

1970. An unofficial woman runner commented about the idea that women shouldn't run long distances: "Women are human beings—not baby mills. Maybe some of these men don't have confidence in their own virility."

❧ ❧ ❧ ❧ ❧

1972. In the inaugural women's run of the Boston Marathon and perhaps with an eye to exhibit both her running prowess and femininity, Kathy Switzer donned a beautiful white tennis dress over a black leotard. After passing the infamous spot where Semple tried to rid her of her number some five years before, she began to overheat and was forced to pull into a gas station to change from clothes that were beautiful to comfortable gear. Grabbing the women's restroom key from the attendant, and a steak knife that customers received when they filled up with a full tank of gas, Switzer made her way to the bathroom. There, in almost total darkness, she stripped down to nothing and begin to cut and mend. Minutes later, she emerged with the tennis outfit pinned up, no legs to her leotard, no socks and an eventual third place finish.

dead, decided to introduce Jock to his sport of choice—the hammer throw. Semple was knocked to the ground and Switzer escaped to change the complexion of the race forever.

After the press had finished with their historical pictures, and Semple and Cloney had returned to the bus which then sped off into the distance, Switzer was left to contemplate her fate. "I was embarrassed and mortified. I was treated like a common criminal when I was only hoping to run a race. The next miles were sad and eerie. Everyone was silent. The only sounds you heard were the quarter-sized snow flakes hitting the leaves of the trees and the runners' feet pounding the pavement."

The fallout from Switzer's landmark run was massive. Will Cloney and Jock Semple were rabid at the post-race press conference. "I am surprised that an American girl would do something like this, and go some place where she wasn't invited," Semple raged.

Katherine Switzer was eventually banned from the AAU on the following four counts:

- *Running without a chaperone*
- *Fraudulent application. Switzer had applied for her number under the name of K. Switzer. (267 out of 700 applicants also used a first initial.)*
- *It was illegal for a woman to run over one-and-a-half mile.*
- *She ran in an all-male race.*

Although it wasn't as monumental as Rosa Parks, Switzer played perhaps the most significant roll in women's sports history.

But this wasn't the first time her athletic prowess had attracted the attention of the press. During the week of the Marathon the year before, *The Boston Globe* ran a story about a woman who was running the half mile for the men's track team at Lynchburg

Kathy Switzer wearing the remodeled tennis outfit—pinned up, no legs to her leotard and no socks.
Photo courtesy of the Boston Public Library Print Dept.

College in Virginia. The story stated that she had some unusual statistics (34-25-37) and that she was going to play the accordion as her talent in the Miss Lynchburg beauty contest later that week. Other interests were listed as tennis, karate and fencing. The woman was Kathy Switzer.

Semple's outrage might be explained by the fact that the first woman runner of the Boston Marathon was actually Roberta Louise Gibb of Winchester, Massachusetts who ran the race without a number the year before. Semple chose to ignore her, though his blood pressure increased measurably when the post race press became more interested in this woman runner that the actual winner Kenji Kimihara of Japan. Gibb finished 124 out of 416 runners.

*Roberta Gibb repeated her trek of 1966 in the following year's race. This time people were well aware of her presence. Erich Segal, an Assistant Professor of Classics at Yale University, ran the 1967 Boston Marathon. After finishing the race, he was asked by the **Boston Globe** what he thought of Ms. Gibb's run. "For ten miles I saw nothing but those beautiful legs," replied Erich Segal who would later write the best selling novel Love Story." I should have asked her to dinner."*

The BAA finally swallowed its pride in 1972 and allowed women the opportunity to participate in "their" Marathon. Nina Kuscsik became the first official winner with a time of 3:10:26.

Rosa Mota, the five foot one, ninety-nine pound runner from Portugal and Uta Pippig a thirty- year-old medical student from Unified Germany are currently the queens of the ball with three Women's Open championships each.

MPC: At about the Five Mile mark, I realized I was exceeding my limits by attempting to keep up with Rad, Richie and Michael. I had to let them go. It was a sad necessity. I would have loved to experience the entire event in the companionship with my friends but it was more important for all of us to stay within ourselves. There would be plenty of time after the race to share our stories.

So I quietly fell back to join with runners who run nine minute miles. My new friends included an English-man dressed as a jester, a man with a Scituate shirt, runners Whit and Paul, who had their names on their shirt, and a runner dressed as a cow causing the crowd to "moo" everywhere we went (my friend Jay yelled out when we passed him that this runner had mad cow disease).

Later in the race, as my grip with sanity slipped, I found myself becoming jealous when fans would yell for the other runners after yelling for me. "How dare they! I thought that I was their favorite."

Two time Olympic champion Abebe Bikila and fellow Ethiopian Mamo Wolde follow the signs to Boston in 1963.
Photo courtesy of Boston Public Library Print Dept.

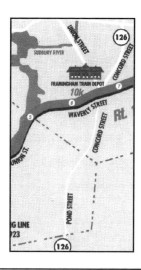

MILE SIX

After passing the Five Mile mark, the runners' brains are full of calculations as they divide five into their time, and then multiply by twenty six. The route has been fairly easy to this point. The pace has been enhanced by adrenaline that fuels the runner for the first 30–45 minutes. Passing this checkpoint, the runners should be ahead of their training runs because of the downhills and excitement. A number of runners, who are new to the Boston Marathon, can fool themselves into thinking that this pace can last for 21 more miles. This will be proven false not far down the road.

At this juncture, the runners begin the first of many tugs of war between mind and body. At the Five Mile mark, runners rejoice over the fact that they have passed the first real benchmark of the race, but at the same time they realize that they haven't even completed a fifth of the course. The devil, on the runners' left shoulder, is starting to tell the angel on the right shoulder, that this might not be their day. With more than 21 miles to go and the easiest part of the course behind, it takes a calm mind and a well-trained body to take the next step and convince one's self that the ten mile mark is just around the corner.

Luckily the crowd starts to increase, because now the runners will need and crave every "looking good" or "you can do it" they can get. At the beginning of the sixth mile, the course moves up and to the right and then levels off through a wooded, residential neighborhood. Halfway through the mile, the course inclines, and swings right. On the left, people may step out of the Italian restaurant LaCantina's, chewing on a meatball and wishing the runners well.

After bending right, the runners get a brief respite with a short descent past a commercial area before another right-hand bend and a slight grade upward at 5.8 miles. Through this section there are trees that provide some temporary protection from either the sun or rain and offer relaxation until the noise from ahead signals a tumultuous welcome around the corner.

Framingham was founded by Thomas Danforth, Esquire. As Deputy Governor of the Colony, he took advantage of his position to gather thousands of acres of wilderness that lay west of Boston. Known to many as Danforth Farms, it was eventually named Framingham after Danforth's home town in England—Framlingham. The town was incorporated in the year 1700.

Framingham became a railroad hub because it was located halfway between Boston and Worcester. In the early-to-mid 1800s, train tracks were laid through South Framingham from Boston because the people on the main stage coach road (now Route 9) didn't want the dirty, noisy train in their area. The railroad was the catalyst for the expansion of this previously wooded area.

Today, Route 135 in South Framingham is primarily a commercial area with a scattering of modest homes. Homeowners spend an average of $150,000 (1995) for a home while store-owners and businesses are paying approximately $10 to $15 per square foot. The town of Framingham stretches 26.44 square miles and has an approximate population of almost 66,000.

In the last two-tenths of the mile, the runners come upon the intersection of Route 135 and Winthrop Street. At this ideal viewing area, people are five or six deep, and draw the runners in like a magnet. They are treated like the guests of honor, but runners must pay attention because that big right turn a half-mile ago is reversed by huge left turn which stretches for a tenth of a mile through this major intersection. This left turn looks like it was molded in this fashion for the sole purpose of straightening out the marathon course. For the next four miles, it will be straight and relatively level.

MILE SEVEN

The first substantial stretch of level and straightforward running begins in the seventh mile. This flat range provides the leaders with the opportunity to feel out their opponents and begin their cat-and-mouse games. Some will initiate a false surge in hope of weeding out the pack, while others will find great comfort in running within the pace of the other leaders.

At the 6.1 mark, Mark Noe, the owner of Mug's Away Pub, is hosting his own form of marathoning. By the time the wheelchair leaders pass at approximately 12:15, this once bikey bar and now converted sports bar establishment, will have had the beer taps flowing for over four hours. They will continue to work them for another twelve.

Mark Noe, who prays for a rainy day in order to keep his patrons belly up and not on the sidewalk, has been a lifetime admirer and spectator of the event. He grew up on the route and was excited about the opportunity to purchase the pub six years ago because of its route location. With cold beers, steamed dogs and public bathrooms, this location is popular with his neighbors and the occasional runner who needs a quick pit stop at this section of the race.

At the 6.2 mile mark, the runners move past the car dealerships of R.H. Long on the right and left of the course.

The Long family has been a commerce leader in South Framingham since the turn of the century. Originally a shoe manufacturer, R.H. Long eventually converted his trade to a product which he thought might be the wave of the future—motor cars. Long manufactured the first Bay State Sedan in the area and sold it for $2,300.

Along with his interest in shoes and cars, R.H. Long ran for Governor of Massachusetts but lost to Calvin Coolidge. R.H. Long's son, Charles, was born around the turn of the century and is the present owner of R.H. Long Auto Sales.

Charles Long and the Boston Marathon are chronological brothers. Over the last nine to ten decades each has grown and prospered. Over that time, the car dealership has taken advantage of Marathon day to throw one of the most entertaining parties on the whole course. On the roof of the dealership a Dixieland band called the Silvano Melchiorri Dixieland Hobo's plays upbeat and Bourbon Street music for the runners and spectators. Across the street, at Long's other facility, another band performs more modern music (recently the Generators). These two dueling bands provide a stereo version of clashing music and tastes. Inside the dealership, youngsters can receive balloons and autographs from some of their favorite race car drivers who have brought their cars for all to see. Radio stations also take advantage of this location to bring live shots to their listeners who are waiting for updates in between their favorite songs. Because of the entertainment and the wide open viewing area, the crowd is stacked into rows of five or six deep, bringing the noise to a level not yet experienced.

MPC: The wondrous nature of the marathon course is evident in the different but equally entertaining segments of the route. From Hopkinton to Ashland and into Framingham the runners seemed to be the entertained rather than the entertainers. Running through Framingham, I found the crowd of thousands in a festive and celebrating mood. Sitting on lawn chairs and standing on curbs, boys and girls, moms and dads, girlfriends and boyfriends, and grandmothers and grandfathers joined together in a generation busting version of "Hot, Hot, Hot" (Ole, Ole, Ole, Ole, Ole"). The singing and clapping brought a great smile to my face and goose bumps on my arms as I and the other runners threw our hands in the air and joined in with the clapping and singing.

1978. At this juncture of the race, the runners settle themselves into packs depending on how comfortable they are at the time. Running through Framingham in the second pack, Jack Fultz experienced a strange phenomenon. "The crowd was really into the race as we moved together as a pack. At one point, the crowd noise rose to such a frenzy that the strength of their enthusiasm caused the pack to surge. The pack was unable to control itself but soon realized that their action was foolhardy. The sudden rush of adrenaline causes a runner's heartbeat to increase by as much as 5%, thus causing consequences somewhere down the road."

1907. The lead pack consisting of ten men made their way across the tracks in Framingham with more than just space separating them from their challengers. Just after the top ten sauntered across the tracks, a freight train moved across Route 135 and cut off 114 runners from the leaders of the race. Two pre-race favorites were caught on the other side of the train with stiffened legs and high blood pressure. Tom Longboat, a member of the lead pack, took advantage of this bizarre twist and ran through the snow to the finish line, the laurel wreath and gold medal.

Some witnesses reported that Longboat actually jumped through an open door on a freight car and out the other side in order to get by the train. In 1973, Harry Augusto, who had witnessed the event, wrote the following account: "I was 14 at the time and the fact that I saw Tom do this has always stayed with me. As I was amazed he took the chance that he did."

Lutz Philip, the temporary leader of the 1973 race, runs past the Framingham train station.
Photo courtesy of Rick Levy.

This type of treatment, usually bestowed upon rock stars and super athletes, was now raining down on some ten-minute milers. It was an amazing feeling.

The route does not deviate and the runners continue to pound the pavement. As they come up on the 6.4 mile mark, it is important for competitors to pay attention to the old railroad tracks that cross the road. Runners, and especially wheelchair competitors, need to maneuver to either the left or right as they pass over the tracks because they are somewhat raised in the middle.

However, Jim Knaub takes a different approach— "Just hit them and hope for the best. It's either your day or it isn't."

At the 6.5 mile mark, on the left side, sits the old train station for the town of Framingham.

Six train routes used to work their way through this station but it has now been converted into a swinging bar called Ebeneezers which hosts a loud and festive marathon party. Like TJ's in Ashland, Ebeneezers takes advantage of the day by setting up outside and inside. Beer distributors provide the tavern with giant balloons with images of their cans or bottles, and the balloons bounce in the wind. With the smell of the barbecue and the outside DJ spinning tunes, runners might ask themselves why they're beating themselves up instead of throwing back a cold one and gnawing on the some barbequed ribs.

On the opposite side of Ebeneezers, is a father and son bakery, named appropriately John and Sons Bakery (est. 1955). John doesn't do much in the line of business except coffee on a cold day. In front of his store, volunteers hand out water to the runners while his driveway is open to cars and vehicles from television stations and spectators. The one-day inconvenience is not a problem for John and his Son because it brings a little life to the town.

MPC: During our winter training runs on Sundays,

1909. Again the train cuts off the runners from the lead pack. One of the pre-race favorites, Robert Fowler, claims he was twice robbed of a potential championship by a badly-timed freight train.

❦ ❦ ❦ ❦ ❦

1988. Two-time winner and pre-race men's wheelchair favorite, Andre Viger, found out the hard way about the hazards of these tracks. Moving smoothly with the lead, Andre didn't attack the protruding train tracks properly and suffered the consequences with a flat tire. When he finally mended the damage, he had lost contact with the lead pack. His lead had disintegrated into an eventual sixth place finish costing him money, glory and a tire. (Some wheelchair competitors have suggested that a truck with spare wheels and parts should follow the competitors to avoid the fate of Andre Viger.)

❦ ❦ ❦ ❦ ❦

1957. Past winner Veikko Karvonen from Finland was running with the lead pack when he was surprised by a woman who approached him with flowers. Karvonen kindly took the flowers, smelled them and continued on with his bouquet in hand. He finished second.

Gerard Cote (left) and Tarzan Brown battle for the lead as they pass the Framingham train station in 1939.
Photo courtesy of Boston Public Library Print Dept.

Rad, Richie, Jack Radley and I would get a ride out to Ebeneezer's in order to train on the course and familiarize ourselves with the route. There we would stretch, and fill up with fluids as curious patrons mosied out from the brunch buffet to watch. The buffet certainly looked more attractive than the 15-18 mile run in slush and car traffic that lay ahead.

John "Jock" Semple is responsible for adding more color and identity to the Boston Marathon than any other individual in the hundred year history of the race. Born in Glasgow, Scotland, he traveled across the sea and took up residence in Philadelphia, Pennsylvania.

A long distance runner who ran in an occasional race, Semple decided to hitchhike to Boston and run the famous Boston Marathon in 1929. He ran that year and eighteen more times, finishing in the top ten six times (best time 2:44:29). Semple eventually made Boston his home and joined the BAA. This marriage between Semple and the Boston Marathon became a successful and passionate union.

With his Scottish brogue and hot temper, he soon became known as the Cardinal of the Boston Marathon, with the unusual ability to make grown men act like first graders being scolded by a nun. Upon calling for an application, Semple was known to loudly demand. "Are you sure you can run twenty-six miles?"

At the first checkpoint area in the 1959 Marathon, a spectator wearing a mask and clown shoes ran out of the crowd and began walking down the route drawing laughs from spectators and runners but not the race director, Jock Semple. Mortified that anyone would try to make a farce out of this temple of running, Semple leaped at the individual, grabbing the mask but missing the comedian. Semple rolled into the gutter with mask in hand while the good-natured runner continued down Route 135 clomping his clown shoes to the delight of many. A policeman on the scene attempted to arrest Semple for assault.

Ken Parker of Canada felt that being the recipient of Semple's wrath was a solemn part of the Boston Marathon experience. "It was an honor to be yelled at by Mr. Semple," he recalls.

Jock Semple will always be remembered for his assault on Kathy Switzer, but without him the race wouldn't be the premiere event it is today. Jock died in 1988 at the age of 84, but many will swear you can still hear his brogue echoing over the hustle and bustle of the pre-race activities.

The 6.5 mile mark has been a traditional checkpoint for the Boston Marathon. The checkpoints provide race officials a set location to monitor the competitors for time and placing at a central location. These checkpoints were initially chosen because of their convenience to a train station. Officials would take the train from Boston to monitor and check the passing runners. Other checkpoints along the race were also determined by the location of the train stations or watering holes for horses. After the hundreds of runners passed, the officials could get back on the train and be in Boston for the finish and the first bowls of beef stew.

These odd distances at which the checkpoints were placed drove some runners crazy because of the difficulty of doing the math for their split times. On the other hand, traditionalists coveted the checkpoint locations because of their historical importance to the race. Eventually the runners won the battle between common sense and tradition, and the checkpoints were moved to five kilometer demarcations and at every mile mark in 1983.

The rest of the seventh mile moves along at the same plateau. The route is almost completely commercial. At the 6.8 mile mark, the runners again have to travel over train tracks. Out of the three sets of tracks, these are by far the most treacherous. Even cars move to the right as they proceed over this obstacle.

On the left side over the tracks are the remains of the brick factory of E.W. Dennison. In 1897 Dennison moved his gum label and box factory from Roxbury to South Framingham. The factory was world famous for baggage labels. Dennison employed over 2000 workers.

The skeletons of these old factories make this section somewhat drab, but the runners are more appreciative of the level topography than the scenery and the fact that this site traditionally provides a helpful tail wind.

The wheelchair runners take advantage of this part of the course to conserve their energy, often coming out of their crouch to take in some of the ambience of the spectators and accompanying parties.

The father and son team of Dick and Rick Hoyt inspire all who witness their quest to meet the challenge.
Photo courtesy of the *Boston Herald*.

MILE EIGHT

This mile signals the end of Framingham and the beginning of the fourth town on the route, Natick. Along the route run the train tracks. In the old days, spectators could watch practically the entire race by boarding the local train to Boston and peering out their window. Sometimes a horsedrawn carriage would get in the way but for the most part the train was the ideal seat. These days there are so many trains traveling to and from Boston that it's not possible for a train to crawl along at a runner's pace.

The eighth mile is mostly wooded, with an occasional house, vacant lot or business. After a third of the mile, Framingham is left behind, and the runners move into the town of the Natick and West Central Street.

The town of Natick is just over 16 square miles and is filled by over 31,000 Natickians.

The name Natick is an Indian word for "place of hills." Native Americans settled in this area with the help of John Eliot who was known as the "Apostle to the Indians." Between himself and the resourceful Native Americans, Natick began to grow and prosper. But soon after, English settlers laid claim to this attractive area and subsequently shipped the "Praying Indians," to Deer Island in Boston Harbor because of the "fear" of retaliation. Once on this barren and ocean exposed island, many of the Native Americans died from the cold and starvation.

The inspiring team of Dick and Rick Hoyt enjoys the level stretches of the course in Natick and takes advantage of the topography to lengthen their strides and open up a little.

Hoyt and Hoyt is not a law firm, but simply a father and son who love and care for each other. Rick Hoyt, the son, was stricken with cerebral palsy as a child. His life centers on the Boston Bruins, Boston University (he was a 1993 graduate), his family and challenges.

Rick loves athletics but his involvement was limited by his disabilitating disease, which restricted his involvement in sports until his father Dick decided to take up running and included Rick in his new passion.

Running around the block pushing Rick in an old wheelchair eventually led to road races, marathons, triathalons and iron man competitions. Dick and Rick were both exposed to a whole new world and in this new world, a new bond formed between the father and son. They now share their pain and triumphs together as a team. As Dick pushed his son through the streets of Hopkinton and all the way into Boston another bond formed—between Team Hoyt and the Boston Marathon.

With this new passion, Rick's sense of humor has blossomed, and it is never more apparent than after each race, when he takes the opportunity to remind his father that he beat him by a second.

"When I'm running" Rick says, "I feel like I've never been handicapped."

2:40:24 is the Hoyts' Boston best.

Mile Eight is generally level until the 7.7 mark. At that point, the route rises for a tenth of a mile before dropping on the other side. Greg Meyer, 1983 winner, points to this incline as a spot in race for a runner to access his/her condition. "You'll have a good idea at this point if it is your day or not. This incline certainly makes an impression on the runners." Some know this slight incline as "Heartburn Hill."

After the limited but trying uphill, the road works its way down. At the bottom of the descent are modest condominiums from which are drawn a gathering of spectators. The West Natick train station is located at the end of this mile.

MPC: In this sometime cynical and unfriendly world, people on the move seem more prone to keeping their

1935. Two Natick policeman, who were working crowd control on motorcycles, were hit by a car which then sped off. Officers Ray Tanner and John Flynn were brought to Leonard Morse Hospital; Tanner had a fractured pelvis and Flynn was released with minor cuts and abrasions. The culprit was never apprehended.

ༀༀༀༀༀ

1950. Yun Chi Choi, from South Korea, was brought to a halt when a red chow dog attacked the Korean runner. After nipping at the sneakers of the runner, the dog seemed satisfied and moved on his way. Choi continued on to finish third in an all-Korean sweep. His countrymen, Kee Yong Ham and Ki Yoon Song finished respectively in the top two spots.

ༀༀༀༀༀ

head down as they hurry on their way instead of offering a hello and a smile to a passing neighbor. This is not the case with the Boston Marathon and is one reason why it is so special. If only for one day, fellow runners give each other assuring smiles, fans genuinely wish the competitors well and inspire them to go faster and farther, and volunteers maintain a constantly pleasant disposition while providing immeasurable support to the athletes.

Across from the Natick condos, a volunteer was handing out dabs of Vaseline. As a runner came upon the table he reached out and grabbed a gob, and as he moved on his way, he yelled in thanks, "I love you." The volunteer retorted, "I love you too."

As I neared the completion of Mile Eight the crowd became sparse and the scenery limited to the pavement in front of me. My focus began to switch from the blondes, beers and barbeque grills to doubts that I would be able to finish the race.

I was still recovering from an injury to my iliotibial (IT) band muscle on the outside of my left knee. After a month of therapy and a cortisone shot, I had improved but was still struggling. Back around Mile Six, I re-aggravated the injury causing limited extension of my left knee. This left me with one leg that had to stay straight and another leg with a lot of responsibility.

These down periods provided an unhealthy incubator for rambling thoughts. I didn't need an abacus to figure out that I had almost twenty miles left.

In an effort to conserve energy, wheelchair competitors traveling through Framingham in 1996 line up behind one another in order to draft off their fellow competitor. Photo courtesy of David Morey.

MILE NINE

For the wheelchair competitors, drafting becomes a game of cat-and-mouse through the flats from Mile Six to Mile Eleven. It has been estimated that the wheelchair competitors who draft only need to exert 70% of the force and energy than when they are running on their own. Seven-time winner Jean Driscoll takes advantage of this segment to push other members of the lead pack beyond their limits. When it's her time to lead the pack in front, she pulls the drafters at a superior speed. This forces the other members of the pack to push past their limits, which often leaves them low on energy when they approach the infamous hills 10 miles down the road.

For the last three miles, the runners have been treated to a pancake course that allows them to settle into a consistent pace without downshifting and upshifting. Mile Nine, on the other hand, hits the runner like a sneaky uppercut with inclines at the beginning and again towards the end of the mile. The route at this point is a combination of commercial enterprises and wood lots. Just past the halfway mark, the runners move pass Natick Auto where the owner, Charles Ribicoff, is treating his employees and their families to a barbecue meal of hamburgers, hot dogs and sausages and an opportunity to cheer on the competitors.

Moving past the dealership and up to the Speen Street intersection (named after the John Speen, a native American who first built on this land in the early 1700s), the runners are greeted by the beginning of Fiske Pond on their right and Lake Cochituate on their left. These waterways stretch for the next half mile on both sides into Mile Ten.

The VFW 1274 on the left side marks the end of Mile Nine

*With temperatures approaching 80°, two-time winner Tarzan Brown decided to surrender the 1941 lead so he could take a swim at the nearby Lake Cochituate, so the story goes. Noted track writer, Hal Higdon, reported that he felt this story was a myth made up by **Boston Globe** writer Jerry Nason. Whatever the case there is no question that at this juncture of the race a refreshing dip is more enticing than continuing up the road.*

Ten miles into the race, runners can be tempted by the refreshing sight of Fiske Pond.
Photo courtesy of the Boston Athletic Association.

MILE TEN

Mile Ten begins with a winding right bend at Horseshoe Curve. The road hugs Fiske Pond on the right and train tracks and Lake Cochituate on the left for three tenths of the mile This stretch of the route is best known for working its way through the Henry Wilson Historical District. Even though Wilson has a whole district named after him, he's actually the second most popular citizen of Natick next to Heisman Trophy winner, Doug Flutie.

Wilson was the Vice President of the United States under Ulysses Grant from 1873 to 1875. With only ten months of education under his belt, Wilson came to Natick from New Hampshire as a young man, found employment in a local shoe factory, educated himself by reading over a thousand books in his spare time and then turned his attention to politics. Given the nickname "Cobbler" by his adversaries, Wilson became a U.S. Senator before moving on to the White House. Known as a friend of the soldier and common man, Wilson gave the majority of his assets to the needy and died in office leaving a humble personal estate.

Doug Flutie was a football star at Natick High School before moving on to Boston College where he will forever be remembered for throwing the "Hail Mary Pass" against the University of Miami. That pass won the game for Boston College in the last second of the game. After college, Doug moved to the pros, but had to go north to the Canadian Football League because no one in the NFL would let him throw the ball on first or second down.

MPC: After passing the two waterways, I encountered a rock-and-roll band by the name of Free Lunch jamming away an some obscure front yard on the right. How many small bands can claim they played for 40,000 people?

After leaving an open-aired area at the end of the lake that provides no protection from the April day's elements, the runners work their way up a slight incline towards the warm and protective arms of the trees of West Central Street.

Uta Pippig enjoys this part of the route. "For some reason, I look forward to this small hill. I don't know why—maybe it's the way it twists back and forth. But I know it's up ahead and I am excited to get there."

At the top of the hill, West Central Street (still Route 135), straightens and begins to move through the residential Henry Wilson district. The road is guarded by trees on each side, although over the years the number of trees has been reduced by disease and ice storms. The treetops on each side meet in the middle like a Marine honor guard touching swords at a wedding. In 1909, Lucy Child, a resident of Framingham, described the site as, "a row of stately trees which fling their arms across W. Central Street forming a green roof in the summer and a brown arch in winter."

In the late 1800s and early 1900s, West Central was utilized for buggy rides on Wednesday afternoons in the spring and summer. In the winter, the street was scraped, rolled and roped off so the affluent could race their horse-pulled sleighs from two o'clock to five o'clock each afternoon.

The Henry Wilson Historical District provides the runners with an architectural time capsule as they pass the many celebrated homesteads on each side of the course. Moving past Taylor Street, which is almost halfway through the mile, the athletes come upon the site where the Edward Wolcott's estate once stood. This 21-room mansion, the most impressive property in the town, was better known for the tunnels which ran from the rear of the estate to the Boston/Albany train tracks 100 feet away. During the 1800s, runaway slaves would jump from passing trains and work their way to Wolcott's tunnels where they would receive food and shelter on their way to Canada.

Past the home of the "Father of Anti-Slavery," the runners continue through the Forest Street intersection. On the left, the athletes pass 71 West Central Street. Here Major Daniel Henry Longfellow Gleason resided after serving in Washington during the Civil War. Gleason was famous throughout the town because of his inside knowledge about the Lincoln assassination. Gleason happened to work with an associate who had attended secret meetings where a plot to kidnap President Lincoln was discussed. One of the individuals present at those meetings was John Wilkes Booth. Upon obtaining information about the plot, Gleason warned Lincoln's people, but they remained unconvinced.

After the assassination, under the category "too little too late," authorities turned to Gleason with a plea to help hunt down the culprits. He helped them find Booth, but the others escaped. Gleason died in Natick in 1917.

Bill Rodgers looks forward to the Ten-Mile mark as an opportunity to throw a surge at the pack. This little game can sometimes helps to get rid of pretenders to the crown.

Amby Burfoot, on the other hand, used to enjoy running within the security of the pack. "It's like a comfortable, cozy nest."

Uta Pippig doesn't care if she runs in a pack or by herself. "I am confident in my abilities and what I can do. Although, if in a pack, I respect everyone in that group. I feel a solidarity with the other runners. I appreciate the physical and emotional investment that they have made in order to run in this race. Although I might not know some of the runners in my pack, I must respect them because at that moment they are the same distance from the finish line as I am."

While Bill, Amby and Uta decide if they want to be part of the bourgeois or proletariat class, police in Natick have their hands full with the thousands of fans and athletes who converge on their town. Their biggest jobs are keeping the crowd back and pulling rollerbladers and bikers off the course. Back in the early nineties a biker ran over a runner who had spent the an entire year training for this day. Instead she spent what should have been her most satisfying hour in a Framingham hospital with ice bags on her legs and an unfinished dream in her heart.

Along with crowd control, the police from each town are responsible for coordinating their duties with officers from the surrounding towns. Coordination includes what the race's technical director, Dave McGillivray, calls Plan B.—a contingency plan to put in place should an emergency arise along the course, such as water pipe break or the emergence of an unexpected sink hole or even the threat of a terrorist bomb. Natick's Plan B would re-route the marathon to either Route 9 or Route 30, both of which run adjacent to the marathon route. These routes would give the runners the opportunity to rejoin the race in either Wellesley or Newton. (I'm sure the Technical Committee of the Athletic Congress would have a field day with measuring that route).

Although it is overtime pay for most of the police, loud sirens, screaming kids and overly-excited fans make it a long day. Finally, after months of planning and late night meetings, their job is done until they have to plan the following year's race.

Firemen in Natick, as in other towns, have also worked in conjunction with their neighboring departments to provide coverage on both sides of the route.

Because the runners act as a human wall from approximately 12:30 P.M. to 3:00 P.M., fire trucks have to be divided up to line critical parts of the route.

The Natick fire chief stated that if an emergency did arise which called for additional help on either side of the route, then the race would have to be stopped for safety reasons. Luckily, there have not yet been any emergencies other than a marathoner stopping in at the local station for aid for dehydration or foot blisters.

With 16 miles to go, the runners are revitalized by the sight of the ten-mile sign. They become exhilarated even though they recognize that the course isn't even half finished. Still, it's an opportunity to take satisfaction in having come this far.

For many recreational runners, ten miles is usually a distance where they call it a day. A number of the participants, mostly bandits or non-qualified runners, take advantage of this day to enjoy the start at Hopkinton and put in some exercise. But when the Ten Mile mark rolls around, it's time for a beer and chicken wings instead of water and a Power Bar.

MPC: Situated at the ten mile mark, a sign in a yardparty read, "Shortcut to Boston" with an arrow towards the kegs of beer in their yard. It crossed my mind.

The variety of faces and interesting outfits add a distinct flair and color to the 1996 race. Here, "cowman" passes through Framingham. Photo courtesy of David Morey.

MILE ELEVEN

The runners move through Natick Center at the beginning of Mile Eleven and cross the Route 27 intersection, the spot that used to be the second checkpoint of the race at 10.2 miles. Here, West Central Street becomes East Central Street. The route's grade is level and provides an ideal viewing location for neighbors and townspeople.

Like Hopkinton and most suburban towns, Natick Center has a village-like atmosphere. From a mile away, you can spot the town center by its church steeples, one church for Protestants and one for Catholics. The First Congregational Church, which was built in the 1850s, sits on the left side of the intersection and has a large clock at the top of its steeple.

Bill Rodgers says that the two things that excite runners are people and clocks.

Opposite the Congregational church is the Natick Common. The Common was created in 1856. The Soldier's Monument was built in 1868 to honor 89 Natick soldiers who died in the Civil War. On normal days this area is usually busy with either a concert on the bandstand or teenagers playing hacky-sack.

After the town green, the runners continue on a level path past the police station and the town hall which are positioned on their right and St. Patrick's church on their left.

After working their way towards the end of the mile, the runners approach Nick's. This popular Natick ice cream and hot dog stand is best known for its Saturday night gatherings of 1950 automobiles and Corvettes. Don't pull in there with your father's Chrysler New Yorker because there is a dress code. For years, the Boston Marathon marked the opening day for Nick's. Now it's a year round establishment. Nick's celebrates the day with decorations of balloons and American flags.

Runners in the 1996 Marathon pass through Natick center. Photo courtesy of Steve Rossi.

1919. As he neared Natick Center, a lead runner by the name of Davis had to stop and stuff newspaper in his sneaker in an attempt to stop the bleeding caused by a nail that had punctured the bottom of his sneaker.

1985. As John Kelley ran one of his 61 marathons, a vendor ran up to him and patted him on his back. The vendor was selling buttons with the face of Kelley on the front. Kelley later said "Would you believe it? I'm hurting, and this son of a bitch is trying to make money off me!"

1918. Members of the armed services, participating in a relay team version of the marathon, were ordered to wear their uniforms and boots in order to prove the quality of the issued military garb.

This temporary halt to the marathon was done in an attempt to contribute to the war effort. The BAA, which was committed to providing an athletic event for the men in the armed services, canceled the usual running of the race. In its place, the BAA organized a ten-man relay from Ashland to Boston. Each leg was two and a half miles. The competitors represented different branches of the United States military. The Fort Devens Divisional Team won the race with a time of 2:24:53.

1965. John Marchant, of the North Medford Track Club, wrote "Pass" on the back of his left shoulder and "Don't Pass" on the back of his right shoulder.

1983. After being married on Saturday, Fred and Paula Palka ran the Boston Marathon wearing shirts that read, "Just Married."

Continuing to the Eleven Mile mark, the runners pass the court house and at the 10.6 mile mark, the Natick Battalion Armory, that was built to honor the veterans of the Spanish American War.

Throughout the history of the race, spectators have had great enjoyment from cheering for certain runners because of the affiliation, emblem or cause profiled on the front of the runner's shirt. Over the last century a wide range of causes from "Pro-Life" to "No Nukes" has been represented on the front of sweating athletes from Hopkinton to Boston (I wonder if anyone wore a shirt saying "horse manure smells better than gas fumes" in the early 1900s).

MPC: Richie, Rad and I wore mustard colored shirts with the letters BOB in bold, black letters. Underneath the letters, read "Boston's Official Bandit" with the number 37,501 (the field of numbered runners was 37,500 at the time the shirts went to press).

Runners have always taken advantage of the marathon forum in order to add their personal piece of color to the race's history. Although Jock Semple thought that costumed runners made a circus out of the event, crowds have enjoyed the sight of the characters who have passed by over the years including the Viking, Superman, Groucho Marx, the Blues Brothers, Kermit the Frog and an astronaut. And, of course, there is always a runner who wears a hat which has a beer can extended four inches in front of him, thus providing him something to run for.

The route continues past some stores and Central Street Grill, and through a residential neighborhood to the end of the mile.

Two-time winner and 61-time participant John "Elder" Kelley (#5) runs side by side with competitor Walter Young in 1937. Photo courtesy of Boston Athletic Association.

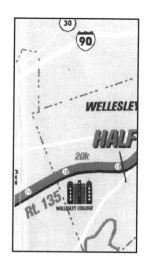

MILE TWELVE

The route continues through Natick and into affluent Wellesley, passing through a mostly residential neighborhood with a sporadic business here and there. House parties are popular and well-wishers are polite. This is the type of mile that can lull the runner into a mode of indifference, but which they would give a million dollars to have back when they are trudging up Heartbreak Hill. As Jim Knaub once noted. "There is no such thing as an unimportant mile."

MPC: During the quiet moments on the course when the sights of lawn-chaired grandfathers diminish and the screams from college kids temporarily subside, you sometimes, unintentionally, find yourself shifting gears from the sightseeing and running on instinct to a drifting focus which occasionally forces you to question your abilities to meet the challenge of the day.

During these lulls in both training and the Marathon, I drew upon the memories of friends and family who have prematurely left this world for a better existence. Friends such as Tom, Billy, David, Henry, Tommy, Tony, Mrs. L., Judy, Dr. Phil, Mike, Michael and Betty all inspired me in my efforts to reach my dream.

These people motivated me because of the fullness of their lives. In a chronological sense, their lives were limited. But during their existence they learned how to appreciate life at a level that most eighty years olds don't. Every snowflake, raindrop, sunrise and breath was appreciated for its beauty. They stared longingly at life and loved and hungered for what it offered. This is why these people are special in my life and why I am awestruck by their courage and their experiences. So as my quads would tighten and my breath would shorten, warm reflections of my earthly departed friends would help me push forward with another step towards my goal.

In the distance, the runners hear a faint echoing of shrill screaming. Veterans of the race realize that they are a mile away from the rallying cries of the women of Wellesley College and a run through a high decibel funhouse.

John Kelley, the patriarch of the Boston Marathon and local hero, talked about the need to stay focused at this juncture of the race. With the impending excitement in the next mile, he believes it is necessary to remind yourself to stay within your gameplan, and not to push yourself too early. He knows from personal experiences that may have cost him two championships: "Running past the girls at Wellesley College, your mind tells you one thing, but your legs do something different. I was always impatient both in life and in running, and it cost me dearly later in the course."

John Kelley, who is best known for running the Boston Marathon over sixty times (he actually dropped out of his first race in Wellesley with blisters), won the race in 1935 and 1945. He finished second seven times and third once.

Kelley was once told by a reporter that if he ran during today's era of prize money and professional races he would have realized more than $500,000 for his 18 top ten finishes. Kelley responded, "Different times, different values. I ran for the love of it. My good friend Ted Williams, baseball's greatest hitter, was asked the same question. This question reminded Williams of the time that he begged Red Sox owner Tom Yawkey to cut his $70,000 contract because he had a sub-par year. We both had a passion!"

Without prize money, Kelley worked several different jobs, including painting houses and working for Boston Edison. Widely loved and admired throughout the running community, he is a member of the Track and Field Hall of Fame and has competed in more than 1500 races from Boston to Japan. The five-foot, three inch, 145-pound runner will forever be linked with the Boston Marathon because of his accomplishments and his love and respect for the race.

Leaving Natick, which is halfway through the mile, the runner is guided east by the same train track that escorted the founders of the race, a century ago. At the 11.7 mile mark, you bid Natick a fond adieu, and enter beautiful Wellesley.

The Wellesley Historical Society retains several accounts of the history of the town. In these writings, the following was noted about the town in the 1800s. "Wellesley was getting a reputation as a town that gets what it wants. Might was right. There was no problem too big [that couldn't] be solved with money."

The town was named after Isabella Pratt Wells, the wife of the town's largest benefactor, Horatio Hollis Hunnewell. Along with donating his wife's maiden name, Hunnewell also provided Wellesley, which was the old West Needham area, with much land and financial support.

Executive Secretary of Wellesley, Arnold Wakelin, spoke for the town with regard to the Marathon: "We are proud to host the race and the halfway point. The Marathon acts as a precursor to spring and good weather. With the contribution from the BAA we are fully capable of living with any inconveniences. On a personal note, it is amazing to see the runners still coming by, one and two hours after the winners have finished."

As the runners pass into Wellesley, the road widens to four lanes, and the speed limit for vehicles increases from thirty-five to forty-five miles per hour. The road drops for two tenths of a mile until the Twelve Mile mark.

Three-time champion Les Pawson (left) and two-time winner Johnny Kelley were both fan favorites in the 1938 race because of their running skills and the fact that they both hailed from New England.
Photo courtesy of Boston Public Library Print Dept.

The average home in Wellesley is a three or four bedroom colonial, on a lot of 10,000 to 15,000 square feet with a price tag of close to $400,000. Shopowners in the town can pay as much as $40 a square foot in order to peddle their trade. The tax rate in 1886 was $9.50 compared to $10.04 for every $1,000 of assessed property in 1995.

The town is spread out over 10.49 square miles, and is occupied by more than 26,000 citizens with an average household income in excess of $79,000.

MPC: As we finished Mile Twelve, a fan yelled out that Uta Pippig had just won. Many, of the male runners started to chant, "Uta, Uta, Uta!" I wondered if they admired her running ability or her blond hair, pleasant face and wonderful disposition. Little did they know, at the time, how she had struggled to overcome adversity throughout the race in order to wear the laurel wreath.

Earlier we had found out that Cosmas Ndeti, from Kenya, had lost to his countryman, Moses Tanui. It was sort of a letdown to the runners. The people of Boston had adopted Cosmas as a brother. But Ndeti has had his time. Now, there is another hero in Kenya.

With more than 14 miles to go in the race, it was best not to focus on the fact that some fellow competitors were relaxing with medals around their necks and you still had over two hours of work in front of you.

As an athlete that worked hard to prepare for this event, I find it mind boggling to realize that there are athletes who can run so fast for so long. I didn't know whether to respect or envy their super-human ability. But either way, it's never more apparent than at this point in the race that the light of the Lord's gracious hand shines on the 2:10 marathoners, while the cloud of a plodder hovers over the sweaty non-endorsed hacker somewhere back in Wellesley.

Of course, with Wellesley comes the decibel-defying divas of the local college who sit in waiting right up the hill from the twelve mile mark. So put in your ear plugs and stay within yourself because here they come.

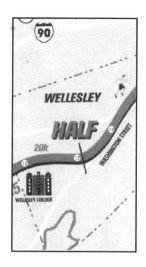

MILE THIRTEEN

The sirens sing their song. The ultimate beauty of the Boston Marathon, along with being the granddaddy of all races, is the way the route takes on a life of its own. Mile Thirteen is a story within the story, and provides further identity, history and uniqueness to the mecca of all marathons. Part of that wonderful identity is Wellesley College. The school is renowned as a fine educational institution, boasting such graduates as First Lady Hillary Rodham Clinton, journalist Diane Sawyer, Secretary of State Madeline Albright and Katherine Lee Bates (class of 1880) and author of "America the Beautiful."

Founded in 1870, this all women's school with an approximate enrollment of 3000, costs each student $25,810 a year to live and learn. A century ago, 704 students paid less than $250 per person to be similarly accommodated.

In the late 1800s, there was a four-story shoe factory situated near the Wellesley College campus. Horatio Hunnewell did not feel that this type of industry was good for the image of the town. So, he simply bought the factory and donated the land to Wellesley College for dormitories.

Currently the college is the town's largest employer with over 1,200 workers.

Although the school's primary focus is one of higher education, Wellesley College is best known to marathoners for being the high-water mark on the course in the shrieks and screams department.

Since the first race in 1897, the women of Wellesley College have hurried through lunch in order to stand on the old stone wall outside Cazenove, Pemeroy and Munger Halls in time to encourage, inspire and often deafen the athletes who are attempting to meet the marathon challenge.

Uta Pippig, "I appreciate the support we receive as we pass the College. I don't let it excite me to the point of

Les Pawson tries to focus on the duty at hand as he runs past the women of Wellesley College in 1940.
Photo courtesy of Boston Public Library Print Dept.

Because Wellesley College has had such an important place in the race, it has always received extensive coverage by the *Boston Globe*. The following represents the *Globe*'s accounts, of the atmosphere and events which occurred at Wellesley throughout the history of the race.

__1897.__ As the runners passed Wellesley College, several young girls received the runners.

__1898.__ The girls cheered for Grant of Harvard.

__1899.__ A bevy of beautiful girls are gowned in fashionable varicolored gowns sitting on a stone wall.

__1916.__ In the hill leading up to Wellesley College, the fair collegians stood along the road within the grounds. They smiled at runners but only a few (students) took notice of the men following in motor cars who tried to get a flirtatious twinkle.

__1928.__ The girls gave a cheer. Runner Joie Ray came along and smiled and laughed at the students. He was seen to wink once or twice, but he kept going as girls smiled—he ended up collapsing at the finish.

__1934.__ Leaders passed the Gothic Building of Wellesley College where the fair undergraduates turned out by the hundreds to applaud the laboring runners.

__1943.__ No girls - Easter vacation.

__1970.__ Wellesley College students were following more serious pursuits. There was scarcely a girl in front of the College.

__1977.__ Vin Fleming, a dishwasher at the Eliot Lounge, thought it was a bigger thrill to pass the girls at Wellesley College than to finish fifth.

running faster than my capabilities. I use it more as a boost to my energy level which I can then utilize somewhere later in the race."

Although the women of the college cheer indiscriminately for all of the runners, the sound is at its highest pitch for the female competitors. In an effort to thank the students for their contribution to the race, several female champions approached John Hancock Financial Services prior to the 1995 race to request that they organize an event at the college. They did, and the rally called "Women on the Move" was held at the Keohane Sports Center on campus. The competitors, who turned out to give thanks included three-time Boston Marathon champion Uta Pippig, of Germany; Olympic Champion Valentina Yegrova of Russia; and New York Marathon Champion Tegla Loroupe, of Kenya. Among the list of distinguished speakers was Wellesley's Athletic Director, Louise O'Neil who spoke eloquently about the mission of the college. "There is no limit to what a woman can accomplish if she has confidence in herself and a determination to make her visions and goals a reality. Everyday women from Wellesley College work a little harder and come a little closer to achieving these goals. Members of the college community encourage students to take chances to break down barriers which stand in our way and to embrace success."

*In Jim Fixx's book, **The Complete Book of Running**, he writes: "the modern world's most appreciative marathon fans [are] the girls of Wellesley College."*

Greg Meyer, 1983 winner, explained his runs through the girls of Wellesley as a skin-crawling experience. "In the old days, the girls were on the street and were literally yelling in your ear. They were so loud that you had no idea what your legs were doing. It was impossible to concentrate. I never thought I would

Geoff Smith travels past the crowd of Wellesley College well-wishers.
Photo courtesy of Jeff Johnson.

say that running through hundreds of college girls would be a challenging experience."

Tommy Leonard, from the Eliot Lounge, was quoted in The Boston Marathon:"These girls, I love them when they come out. They're all good looking chicks. I try to make dates. See you at the Eliot Lounge, but none of them show up—I'm 0 for 21."

In 1988, Michael Goldstein was so thrilled running by the female college students that he decided to turn around and do it again.

MPC: By the thirteen mile mark, the anticipated struggle is slowly becoming a reality. The route becomes hilly, and the tough half of the course still lied ahead. So as your head begins to droop just a notch, you gladly come upon this oasis of sound which is utterly amazing.

I arrived at the gates of Wellesley College more than two hours after the wheelchair competitors had passed. I didn't expect much at that time of the day, but I still looked forward to passing the area that veteran runners had talked so much about in the past. As I came upon the campus, I was surprised to see the place still packed with enthusiastic college students. It made me wonder if the admissions department requests applicants to submit high school grades, SAT exam scores and a recording of themselves screaming. To maintain such a level of volume for so long of period must be at least as challenging as running the twenty-six mile course.

Upon this great outpouring of passion, my spirits were lifted, and I felt I owed it to these people to keep working hard. If I were to stop at this point, I would have betrayed their trust, and let them down. The only way I could repay them was to dig in and concentrate on putting one foot in front of the other.

1995. The majority of the Wellesley College students wore tee-shirts which were part of a promotion by Nike; students displayed shirts with their own personal endorsements. One shirt read, "Wellesley girls have been on top for 120 years" and another proclaimed, "Wellesley College is not a girl's school without men but a women's school without boys."

1996. "The cheering began at 12:25 when the first wheelchair contestants began to roll by. It reached a crescendo shortly after 1:00 when the first pack of a dozen male runners approached, and it remained constant for more than three hours."

1966. As Roberta Gibb, the first woman to run the Marathon, passed the students' of Wellesley College, she heard them scream, "It's a woman! It's a woman!" Upon hearing such a passionate response, Gibb said, "It was like I was setting them free."

1996. The rally was again held at Wellesley College before the 100th running of the race. The star of the show was Roberta Gibb. A number of the current world class runners waited in line to obtain her autograph.

Over the years, Gibb has felt somewhat slighted because of the massive attention Kathy Switzer received for her run in 1967. But there is no question that Gibb, in her black top bathing suit, her brother's white Bermuda shorts and a pair of boys size 6 Adidas sneakers, became the trailblazing woman of the Boston Marathon a year earlier in 1966.

Throughout the mile, the runners are sandwiched by train tracks on their left and the Wellesley College campus on their right. From the 12.0 mark to 12.6, the route moves consistently uphill. At 12.7, the route dips before inclining into Wellesley Center. At the figurative door of the town center, the road flattens out to the end of Mile Thirteen.

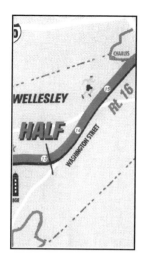

MILE FOURTEEN

Mile Fourteen begins at the end of the upper town center. After two tenths of a mile, you hit a slight decline and subtle twist left. This takes you past an intersection at Grove Street. On the left corner, is a commercial building while on the right is a group of up-scale shops.

For five or six minutes, the women of Wellesley College have silenced that voice in your head that keeps asking, "why are you doing this to yourself." As the runners move deeper into Wellesley Center, they arrive at another psychological landmark on their journey—the halfway point.

The 13.2 mile mark is situated in the middle of Wellesley Center where the runners are squeezed by architecturally-pleasing brick and stucco faced buildings that pose a sharp contrast to the abandoned factories and boarded up buildings that lined the course just a few miles ago.

Uta Pippig, "As you move past the halfway mark, the road narrows. It's not a concern but I am aware of it."

On days other than the one that the Boston Marathon occupies, people can mosey into town and shop for antiques at Swan and Stuart ("where race day is not a good business day. We usually get gum-chewing, ice cream-dripping kids who need to use the bathroom"), cheese at The Cheese Shop, leather goods at London Harness, or a cup of hazelnut java at the local bagel shop. But today the runners are the consumers, and they're only interested in water, oranges and taking another yard off the course.

MPC: At this point of the day, the oranges being offered by well-meaning fans are starting to turn warm. Although I was starving for something that would help alleviate the discomfort, a warm orange actually made my stomach

The lead group of runners works its way through Wellesley Center and past the halfway point in 1994.
Photo courtesy of Victah Sailer.

Women's wheelchair champion Jean Driscoll moves towards her seventh championship in the 1996 Boston Marathon. Only the great Clarence DeMar has as many. Photo courtesy of FayFoto.

turn and began bouts of queasiness that would be magnified over the next thirteen miles by each cookout aroma that crossed the route. So as my stomach turned, I searched for a college friend who told me he would be waiting in Wellesley. Although the odds of seeing him were unlikely, I needed to see him. The shouts from Wellesley College were wearing off.

The runners continue past the town hall and a small duck pond on their left. On the right, up ahead at the half mile mark, is the end of Route 135. The runners follow the green sign that reads "Route 16 East—Cambridge/Boston." Following a left fork, the runners move past St. Paul's Church on the right. On the left, the runners move by a rock that commemorates the first ever high school football game. Wellesley beat Needham 4-0 on November 30, 1882.

At this spot on the course and continuing for the next mile, wheelchair competitors have noticed an unusual and inhibiting bumpy grade to the road. Women's wheelchair champion Jean Driscoll noticed, "For some reason, you can't stroke fluidly at this section which causes you to have to bear down more than you should through a level section."

Jean Driscoll holds the longest consecutive winning streak in the history of the Boston Marathon. From 1990, (when she felt she didn't belong in the starting line) through 1996 and still counting, Jean has worn the laurel wreath with pride. She looks to Boston as the ultimate event—"bigger than the Olympics!"

She begins her training schedule at the University of Illinois (a trailblazing institute in the study, training and teaching of disabled athletes) where Jean pushes herself to her limits by increasing the ever important strength-to-weight ratio. In preparing for 1996, the 112-pound champion bench pressed 200 pounds. This strength will give her the physical and mental ability to attack the hills instead of fearing them.

Two weeks before the race, Jean moves to the south shore of Massachusetts in order to take advantage of the area's hills and topography.

Jean is the current world record holder with a time of 1:34:22. After winning the Boston Marathon a couple of years ago, Jean was invited to run with President Clinton. Clinton remarked, "You have the best-looking arms in America."

Mile 14 has witnessed several interesting runner-spectator confrontations. In 1901, a local man on a bike became a hero when he raced up alongside a riled horse and grabbed him by the bridle seconds before he trampled the oncoming runners. In 1922 as a car turned on to the marathon route, it just missed leader Clarence DeMar. DeMar was so infuriated that he took a swing at the driver. He missed the driver, but hit a passenger in the stomach. DeMar spent the next mile looking over his shoulder for a potential retaliation.

As the mile continues, the road proceeds along a slight rise into a commercial neighborhood before it levels off at the end of the mile.

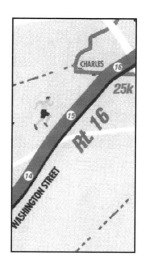

MILE FIFTEEN

This is truly the calm before the storm. The last "placid" mile to work out any remaining cramps and the time to adjust game plans to accommodate on the runner's physical condition, recent splits and the weather. After this mile ends, the runner realizes that the first fifteen miles were nothing but a dress rehearsal. From this point forward, the ring announcer is yelling, "Let's get ready to rumble!"

At the beginning of the mile, Hunnewell Park runs along the right-hand side of the course. The train tracks on the left lead to the Wellesley Hills train station and the local Post Office at the half-mile mark. After the train station, there are various shops and commercial buildings on the right, and on the left are the Unitarian Universalist Societal Church and the 65-foot Wellesley Hills Clock Tower built with the famous Wellesley fieldstone. In years past, bells of the tower used to be rung to greet the runners, but the increase in the magnitude of the running field over the past decades has made it impractical to keep ringing the bells.

As the mostly level mile ends, you approach a multi-street intersection with stores on both sides. One of the stores, on the left, is relevantly called Marathon West. Here they take advantage of their namesake event to hand out Power Bars and to fit sneakers on individuals who have pledged to run the race next year.

Up ahead, the runners must fork left and continue on Route 16 East. This takes the athletes by a bridge over Route 9. At the beginning of the bridge, there is a substantial bump.

Across the bridge, the Wellesley Hills Congregational Church stands on the left. On the right there are some small shops. The mile then turns residential and shaded for one last level section.

After running 15 miles in 1996, Denise Schwabb and Ed Walters stopped to exchange wedding vows at the Wellesley Hills Congregational Church. Said the Reverend Craig Adams, "To run this far was an effort, but the contest you

As the runners pass the town clock in Wellesley in the 1994 race, they quickly approach the topographic nightmares of the Boston Marathon. Photo courtesy of Victah Sailer.

Four-time winner Bill Rodgers (right) runs stride for stride with the notorious Jerome Drayton in 1975.
Photo by Jeff Johnson.

face beyond the finish line is going to be even greater." The happy couple kissed, and moved back on the course to finish the race.

At this section of the race, four-time winner Bill Rodgers again assesses his situation and adjusts his game plan. With the steepest downhill of the race approaching in the next mile, good downhillers like himself begin to ready for the assault.

Boston Billy and John Kelley are the local favorites of the racing population. Rodgers is almost single-handedly responsible for sparking America's love affair with running. His triumphs in 1977–1978, when he won the triple crown of marathoning (New York, Fukuoka and Boston) in the span of six months, was truly one of the great athletic feats of all time.

As a college student at Wesleyan University, Rodgers roomed with 1968 Boston Marathon winner, Amby Burfoot. During college and after graduating, Rodgers took an indifferent approach to his running. At one point, he actually gave it up.

Smoking a half pack of cigarettes a day and drifting between jobs, Rodgers was forced back into running when his motorcycle was stolen. With no other way to make his way back and forth to his job, Rodgers transported himself with his feet. Running to and from work and anywhere else he wanted to venture, Rodgers regained his passion for the sport and eventually won his first of four Boston Marathons in 1975 while living off food stamps.

The running mania that he ignited eventually provided a comfortable living for Rodgers. He currently owns the Bill Rodgers Running Center in Fanueil Hall, and appears throughout the world at running clinics and expos.

Famous for his swinging left arm and gloved hands, the 5'9", 128-pound Rodgers will forever be linked with the names of the other Boston sports greats Larry Bird, Ted Williams and Bobby Orr.

MPC: Training on the marathon course has its good and bad points. The runner who is unfamiliar with the course probably enjoys Mile Fifteen because it's level and relatively lenient. But for the runner who is already oriented to the course, it becomes a mile of fear. When this mile is completed, there are no breaks, no fun, no high-fiving fans, no dancing to the music from house parties—just outright pain.

With just a half-mile left in the town of Wellesley, I still haven't found my college friend. I really need to see a familiar face to pump me up, and I keep looking.

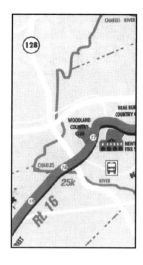

MILE SIXTEEN

As Mile Fifteen turns into Mile Sixteen, the race experience becomes a little like a visit to the dentist. You feel a little pain at the moment, but you know that very soon you're going to experience some real pain.

Up to this point, the elite runners have been like boxers feeling each other out in the early rounds—now it is showtime.

When I think of the beginning of Mile Sixteen, I'm reminded of the time when I was somewhat younger sitting at the peak of a roller coaster ride with my friend Steve Alperin. As we anxiously waited to plummet back beneath the clouds, Steven closed his eyes and made peace with his maker. I punched him in the arm and yelled at him to throw his arms up in the air.

The descent starts in Wellesley and lasts almost half a mile to Newton Lower Falls. This radical drop brings the runners to 55 feet above sea level—a 100-foot drop in all. The downhill course moves past the Warren School and Field on the right and some small businesses on the left. At the bottom of the hill the road crosses the Charles River by way of a small bridge. (The Charles River also begins in Hopkinton and ends in Boston—but that route is 80 miles).

Although this hill is less publicized than other sections of the course, it is a cause for great strategy. Bill Rodgers attacks here while others derive their own personal strategy. Uta Pippig confides, "How I approach this section of the course is my own little secret."

Except for the occasional surges and cat-and-mouse games through the flats of Framingham and Natick, this represents the first real strategic spot in the race. Good downhillers take advantage of this spot to roll. A surge will hopefully separate them from the other leaders before getting to the hills in the next miles.

For wheelchair competitors, this downhill is critical because of the strategy involved and danger of the topography. As these competitors work downhill, they must proceed with caution. Some push the envelope and attack this section of the course at speeds approaching 40 miles per hour, but depending on weather conditions, crowd control and the quality of the street, a hell-bent style can be dangerous if not done properly.

A 100-foot drop, over a half mile, can mean problems for the legs and arms of competitors who have just finished fifteen highly-paced, adrenaline-filled miles. This cause and effect can be similar to body shots in the early rounds of a boxing match.

After making it to Newton Lower Falls, some runners probably feel as though they should wave their hands above their heads like the surfacing Acapulco cliff divers do in order to let the spectators know that they are all right.

Moving past some stores, the runners approach the last quarter of the mile. The street widens to five lanes, allowing the runners to spread out and the spectators to get a good look at the athletes.

Bill Rodgers on the downhills of the Boston Marathon, "If you want to win Boston, you must be a good downhiller. You need to practice downhills."

Grete Waitz, four-time New York Marathon winner, had to drop out of the Boston Marathon with the lead just a few miles away from the winner's circle. She gained great respect for the downhills of Boston. "I never train downhill. No one I know trains downhill—we only train uphill. It can be hard to run downhill. Next year I'll be ready." (She never came back).

Dr. David Martin, a physiologist at Georgia State University, has studied the effects of downhilling versus uphill running. He stated that downhill running takes more out of a runner because the dual need to

1897. John McDermott, from New York, made his move on the downhill leading into Newton Lower Falls and never looked back en route to the championship of the first Boston Marathon.

1898. As Louis Liebgold ran down into Newton Lower Falls, in tenth place, he caught his heel on the train tracks which ran down the middle of the street. He crawled over to the side of the road where he was eventually picked up and taken to Boston.

1961. For the last two to three miles, a black Labrador running along the sidewalk matched the leaders stride for stride. When the leaders and dog arrived at Newton Lower Falls, the dog darted on to the road. Eino Oksanen of Finland leaped over the dog, but John Kelley (younger not related to the elder) was knocked to the ground. English runner Fred Norris stopped and helped Kelley to his feet. Oksanen never looked back and ran on to victory.

At the press conference after the race, Oksanen laughingly said, "The dog should have been shot." John Kelley thought of the irony of an Englishman sacrificing his dream in order to aid an Irishman and reflected, "What a wonderful representative of his country."

1969. Scandinavian champion Pentto Rummakko of Finland was close to the leaders as he ran through Newton Lower Falls. As he focused on each step, a fan by the name of Paul Cahill from Wellesley came out of the crowd and punched Rummakko in the chest knocking him to his knees. Off duty Newton policeman, Richard Gunn, arrested Cahill while Rummakko picked himself up and finished seventh.

run and brake uses a variety of muscles. Even the recovery is effected. "It takes many more weeks to recover from Boston [Marathon] because of the delayed muscle soreness caused by chronic eccentric downhill loading."

Runners such as Alberto Salazar, Dave Beardsley, Greg Meyer, Rob de Castella and Craig Virgin have never been the same after pushing themselves at Boston.

Dave McGillivray, a veteran marathoner and the race's technical director, felt that the ability to withstand the physical punishment of the downhills depends on the type of runner. "If you land like a helicopter, then the course can beat the heck out of your quads, knee joints and feet."

When the TAC ruled the Boston Marathon ineligible for any American or world records, they stated the severe drop in elevation allowed for easier downhill running thus making record times less of an achievement. This raised the eyes of many veterans of the race. They argued that its the downhill running that beats up the competitors. The act of braking and advancing at the same time is as severe as running any flat course.

At the bottom of the hill and the end of the mile, the runners catch their breath just in time to start what some consider the ugly sister of the Newton Hills.

MPC: The injury to the outside of my left knee was severely tested on the downhills. The inability to roll the knee over was a painful undertaking during this hundred foot drop. My left leg had to be extended straight, like a peg leg, while my right leg did the rolling.

At this point in the race I've stopped checking my splits. Time isn't a factor. From here on it's just survival.

With the bottom of the hill in sight, I spotted a young girl with oranges on the right side of the course. I needed something, but I didn't want to waste the steps it would take to deviate to the side of the road. So I yelled to her to throw it. She misjudged the distance and the orange sailed behind me. With a dire need to eat the orange, I threw my left hand behind me and made a behind-the-back catch that would have made Ozzie Smith smile.

Just as I snared the orange and the Route 128 hill stood before me, a fan ran on to the course. It was my college friend Jim Delaney. He had a beer bottle in one hand and glow on his face which made me jealous. He ran with me for a hundred yards and asked me how I was doing. I answered, "I feel like shit, but I'll do it." As he turned off he yelled "You're the man! Go get 'em!"

Although I was psyched to see him, I was equally disappointed when we parted company. The pain and misery I was experiencing were made more difficult by the solitary aspect of marathoning. It was a lonely pain.

But his thoughts were enough motivation to get me over the hill to my parents who would be waiting in front of Newton-Wellesley Hospital.

The lead group in 1995 bids good-bye to Wellesley and enters Newton.
Photo by George Martell/*Boston Herald*.

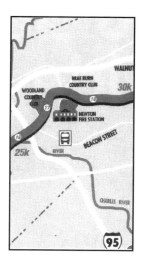

MILE SEVENTEEN

From the beginning of this mile to the halfway mark, the runners get to test out their quads, which just went through the spin cycle on the last downhill.

At the start of the mile, the runners move past the Baury House. Built in 1755 by shipbuilders, it faced old Natick Road until it was recently remodeled as a professional building and turned to face the perpendicular road. The architect was obviously not a running fan.

At the base of the hill on the right sits Gregorian Rugs. As with any successful business, it is important to exploit your surroundings and events of stature in order to market your product. The people of Gregorian Rugs agree with that theory and take advantage of the Boston Marathon to both enjoy the race and sell rugs. During Marathon week, Gregorian has a special sale on carpet runners for hallways and stairways. Outside they hang a sign depicting a marathoner in order to remind potential consumers of the ongoing sale. During the day, 40,000 living and breathing reminders will pass the store.

Two tenths into the mile, the five lanes become four lanes that are split by cement islands. A sign on the right welcomes runners to "Newton, The Garden City." On the right, they pass a pre-Civil War home, now a restaurant named the Pillar House, and then proceed over a bridge spanning Route 128 and Interstate 95. If the runners wanted to take a right onto Route 128, and if in condition to do so, they could wind up in Florida. A left would take them to Maine.

Although the three hills ahead on Commonwealth Avenue get the most attention, this stretch over Route 128 is recognized by some as the most difficult challenge for the entire course. For almost three-quarters of a mile, a gradual ascent causes the runner to feel depleted a little earlier than planned. Wheelchair competitors, in particular, pay keen attention here to their pace and plan of attack. Wind can be a factor during the run over this wide open bridge.

Two-time winner Geoff Smith observed, "This extended uphill, coming off a downhill, is an example of the reverse muscle usage which beats the hell out of the runners' legs."

After scaling the hill, a 55-foot rise in elevation over a half-mile long, the runners work their way up to another cement island at a set of traffic lights.

At this juncture, the hill begins to peak. On the right is Newton-Wellesley Hospital founded in 1881 as one of the country's first "cottage hospitals," so named because each cottage occupied by patients with a common infectious disease.

All hospitals across the country are required to have a disaster plan in place in the event a catastrophe strikes. Every year, the disaster plan must be rehearsed on two separate occasions. For Newton-Wellesley Hospital, the chaos of the Boston Marathon meets requirements analogous to earthquakes, flood, and nuclear attack; thus, this day has been designated as one of the hospital's two disaster drills. Doctors, local police, firefighters, nurses and hospital social workers rehearse their catastrophe plan. It is a practice drill that has practical application on Marathon day because the hospital is a primary source of first aid for both runners and spectators.

In addition to providing health care services for their patients, hospital personnel have been known to sneak a peak at the proceedings. Such was the case many years ago when a maternity ward nurse was scheduled to work on Marathon Day. It just so happened that her boyfriend was running the race, and the supportive girlfriend/ nurse felt compelled to watch the race in hopes of catching sight of her loved one. While she watched, she held a five-day-old baby who seemed equally interested in the proceedings. The baby's name was Jerry Nason. As a boy, he became a volunteer lemon carrier for the race and later, a sports writer for the Boston Globe. *Nason covered the race for over a half a century. Nason's love and passion for this event is another ingredient in the Marathon's folklore. People like himself and reporter Lawrence Sweeney, who covered the race in the early decades, have provided the important bond that will forever join participants from the 1897 race to all races that follow.*

The runners move on a declining grade past the hospital. On the left, sits the Woodland Country Club which was built in 1897 to offer recreational activity for vacationers at the posh resort Woodland Park Hotel a mile down the road.

Its beautiful clubhouse, which burned down in both 1910 and 1983, is situated down the driveway about a five iron from the road. The course was designed by the famous golf course architect, Donald Ross.

The current manager says that the club doesn't do anything special for the day. "In reality," he confessed, "the race is a nuisance. We can't book any events for the day, and the streets are shut down from early morning to late afternoon. Some members play golf in the morning, have lunch, and then take in the race from the club grounds. But in general, the day is more an inconvenience than anything."

A number of Newton residents used to claim that the race should be called the Newton Marathon because it hosts a longer portion of the race than any of the other seven towns—almost six miles. Within those six miles lie a hospital, two colleges, two country clubs, one town hall and four hills. Arguably, more races have been won and lost in this town than in any other town along the route.

Jon Anderson (left) and Tom Fleming (right) are escorted by the police and bikers during the 1973 Boston Marathon as they work their way up the overpass which crosses over Route 128. Photo by Rick Levy.

Once a part of Cambridge, Newton was known as New Towne in the late 1600s; upon being separated from Cambridge, it joined words and dropped the "e."

The town of Newton boasts a population of over 80,000 people. It is 18.22 square miles wide and has an approximate median house price of $290,000. It is perhaps best known for being the home of the Fig Newton, the third most popular cookie in the country which was created in 1891 by baker James Henry Mitchell.

The late Mayor of Newton, Theodore Mann, was always concerned with the cost of sponsoring such a large event. At the same time, he felt the town of Newton had a historical obligation to make it happen.

Newton Mayor Thomas Concannon echoes these thoughts when he described the race as a cultural event that provides a carnival and reunion type atmosphere for the people of his town. "It's a coming out party. After a long New England winter, people get out of their houses, and reintroduce themselves to one another." He went on to draw a comparison between the race and a recent visit by Mother Theresa. "It's culturally enriching. The town benefits in many ways which far outweigh the monetary costs."

Newton takes advantage of the long weekend to plan a number of special events. On the Sunday of Marathon Week, the town hosts a one mile run for children.

As the runners move past the Woodland Country Club, the local Green Line trains have dropped off their passengers at the Woodland train stop across the street. This area takes on double duty for the day as both a train stop and viewing area.

The end of the mile turns residential and flat for one last breather before the road turns the corner up at mile eighteen.

1967. As Kathy Switzer approached the intersection before Newton-Wellesley Hospital, she spotted a policeman who was suspiciously eyeing her. She turned to her coach Arnie Briggs and told him, "If this cop tries to arrest me, I'm going to resist arrest. I haven't come this far for nothing." So Switzer boldly moved up to the point where the cop was standing, where he turned toward her with a stern expression and said, "Your hands look cold. Take my gloves."

Switzer went on to finish the race while making history.

❧❧❧❧❧

1909. The two leaders, Lewis Fine and Louis Tewanina, pride of the Hopi tribe of Arizona and school friends of Jim Thorpe, pushed themselves beyond their limits in the 90° weather. Their inevitable collapse gained them a bed at Newton-Wellesley Hospital.

❧❧❧❧❧

1911. A *Boston Globe* reporter covering the marathon, drove by the Newton-Wellesley Hospital and wrote this the following day: "It's a pathetic sight to see invalids and convalescents waving to these sturdy athletes."

With white running gloves tucked neatly into my waistband, I approach the spot where my parents are standing. I had to figure out whether to keep running or to stop and assure myself a ride home.
Photo by John Connelly, Jr.

MPC: As I ran up the hill over Route 128 with the image of condensation slowly dripping down the side of Jimmy's beer still in my mind, I started to get excited about seeing my parents a half mile ahead. At this point, I realized I was experiencing a vulnerability that I never would have imagined in a road race. The thought of seeing my parents provoked tremendous emotion. I suddenly found myself crying as I reflected about all they had done for me in my life.

As I finished the first of the four hills, I could see my parents a hundred yards down the road. My mother had a maternally concerned look on her face while my father took a step out on to the course to take some pictures just like the old days during birthdays, first communions and graduations. As I passed them, they asked how I was doing, and stretched out a bottle of Gatorade. I told them I was all right, and waved off the drink. My father gave me the thumbs up, and my mother waved, and again I was all alone.

After I passed my parents, a strange thought came to my mind. I realized that I might have missed out on an opportunity to get a ride home. The last thing I wanted to happen was to be passed out on someone's front lawn and have some BAA official walk by shaking his head and saying "Bandit."

WOODLAND PARK HOTEL,

WASHINGTON STREET, CORNER WOODLAND ROAD,

AUBURNDALE.

JOSEPH LEE, Proprietor.

This New and Elegant Hotel is now open for the reception of Guests at all Seasons
of the year. Steam Heating during the Winter Months.

BOWLING ALLEYS, BILLIARD AND POOL ROOMS

OPEN TO THE PUBLIC.

JOSEPH LEE, Caterer.

ICE CREAM, FANCY CAKE, AND DELICACIES
MADE TO ORDER.

Mr. Lee will attend to the Catering for Parties, Weddings, Etc., in Newton or
Boston; has unrivaled facilities for giving Dinner Parties, Game Suppers,
Etc., at his Hotel. Ice Cream delivered in any part of Newton.

An 1896 advertisement promoting the Woodland Hotel bragged about its ability to deliver ice cream anywhere in Newton. Illustration courtesy of the *1896 Newton Registry.*

MILE EIGHTEEN

The route is level for the first two-tenths of a mile as the runners approach the turn from Route 30 onto Route 16 east. On their left before the turn, the runners proceed past the spot where the old Woodland Hotel used to stand.

Back in the late 1800s and early 1900s, the Woodland Hotel was frequented by the affluent of Boston. These well-to-do Bostonians would make the trip from the city by horse and carriage. Along with the Yankees from Boston, President Taft and over the weekend of the big game against Harvard, the Yale football team used to grace this hotel with their presence.

At one time, the hotel was owned by Newton socialite named Joseph Lee. Lee was the son of slaves in Charleston, South Carolina. As a young man he had witnessed the bombing of Fort Sumpter that signaled the beginning of the Civil War. Along with the hotel, Lee ran a very successful catering business and owned a patent for a breadcrumbing machine.

In 1917, the hotel was bought by Lasell College though the school was unable to use the facility in the first year because Newton-Wellesley Hospital had commandeered the property during the influenza epidemic. In 1952, the property was sold to a contractor who built 27 houses on the site. This location used to be the fourth checkpoint for the race before they were switched to even intervals in 1983.

At the 90° turn from Route 16 onto Route 30 and Commonwealth Avenue sits the Newton Fire Station. Many runners look to this spot as another landmark on their long list. Aware that the hills lie ahead, you finish up on Route 16 like an extricated boater floating helplessly toward a waterfall.

The Newton Fire Station, located on the right corner of the intersection, is conveniently situated for viewing the race, providing the firefighters with the opportunity to look out on to the level end of Route 16 and then cross the room to the Route 30 side to witness the start of first hill.

In case of an emergency, fire personnel keep fire apparatus on both sides of the course in order to protect citizens on either side of Newton. The fire engine sitting on the carriage road across the street quickly becomes a carnival ride for bored kids.

Hot days means business for locations such as fire stations and hospitals. On these days, the first aid line can stretch far with the amateur runners needing the most help. At this spot in the race, it is not uncommon to see runners still passing by six or seven hours after the sound of the starting gun.

MPC: I used the turn at the fire station as a gauge for estimating how I might fare in the coming miles. In past training runs, I approached this spot in a variety of physical states that usually forecast the eventual success or failure of my run. If I was struggling at this juncture, it would be early exit. Other than my knee and nausea, I was feeling pretty decent. My wind was strong ,and my wife, son and friends were two miles ahead.

At this point, my friends Richie and Rad had stretched the distance between myself and them to almost 20 minutes. While I ran, I would occasionally overhear a spectator say,"There goes another BOB shirt." It gave me comfort knowing they were still alive and kicking. It was as if I had found a strand of their shirt stuck to a branch, somewhere deep in the jungle.

Coming into the race, I felt that they were better prepared than I was. If I had spotted one of them on

1909. *The Boston Globe* wrote, "The long, hard, smooth hills in the distance have proved to be the undoing of many ambitious lads."

1925. Frank Wendling, from Buffalo, New York pulled out of the lead pack to enjoy a hot tea at the Woodland Hotel. He rejoined the snowy race and finished tenth.

1948. Bill Lanigan stopped his run to admire two girls playing tennis at Lasell College. He proceeded to grab a racket and join the girls in a volley before continuing his run which he eventually finished.

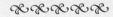

1907. Canadian Charlie Petch was running stride for stride with Thomas Longboat at the turn. Overcome by the excitement of the crowd, Petch danced his way past the corner. Longboat kept his head down and moved on to the championship. Petch finished sixth.

1979. Toshihiko Seko's coach, Kiyoshi Nakamura, informed the press that his runner would stay on Bill Rodgers' shoulder until the fire station where he would then destroy Rodgers on the hills. Rodgers proved to be the destroyer, beating the second place Seko by forty-five seconds.

1972 winner Olavvi Soumalainen takes the turn at the Newton Fire Station
onto Commonwealth Ave. Photo by Rick Levy.

*the side of the road, I would have been demoralized. It would have convinced me that if they couldn't do it—then
I was a goner.*

*Two-time New York Marathon champion German Silva respects the hills, but is more concerned with the five sharp
turns on the course (fire station in Newton, top of Cleveland Circle, bottom of Cleveland Circle, onto Hereford
Street, and onto Boylston Street). "Everybody talks about Heartbreak Hill, but I'm more interested in the corners.
You can take advantage of the corners. If you are prepared, you are prepared for everything."*

The turn on to Commonwealth Avenue is taken with caution and a wide circle complements of tiring legs. Wheelchair competitors approach the corner at speeds of 25 miles per hour. Soon, their downhilling muscles will be taking a break, and their uphill muscles and rotator cuffs will confirm whether or not the competitors spent enough time in the weightroom. The wheelchair competitors, who are on the heavy side, must wait for the downhills to make their move. For the light wheelchair competitors, whom have a high weight to strength ratio, its time to attack.

Just after turning on to Commonwealth Avenue, hill Number One is approximately a half mile with a roundabout swing to the left.

Uta Pippig: "After turning at the fire station, I look forward to seeing the sign on the side of the road that lists the leaders. Every year I look for it. I train with some of the Kenyan men, so I am interested in how they are doing up ahead."

MPC: The first hill's steepness reminded me of a Stairmaster workout or going up a down escalator.

On the left, the runners are boxed in by a grass island which protects a carriage road. This island will continue into mile twenty-two. On the right, at the start of the hill, sits Brae Burn Country Club.

The Club's manager informed me that the members, like the members at the Woodland Country Club, show up early to play a round of golf, grab lunch and work their way out to the street to watch the competitors. Brae Burn attempts to co-exist with their neighbors by allowing some parking and use of bathroom facilities. The day is long and arduous for the club's security staff.

Many years ago, Brae Burn's golf course used to cross over Commonwealth Avenue. So beware of some elderly golfer who lives off interest income and thinks FDR should run for a second term. He might just hit a low seven wood over the race route.

On both sides of the street for the next three to four miles, runners are sandwiched by affluent Georgian estates with values which range anywhere from $400,000 to $1,000,000.

Greg Meyer, the 1983 winner, feels that this hill is the more difficult of the three Commonwealth Avenue hills. "It's steeper and longer than the other two. Heartbreak Hill is a gradual rise which levels off, whereas the first hill at the turn is a real test to your physical condition at this juncture of the race."

After scaling the first of the Commonwealth Avenue hills, by digging down and swinging left, the runners have a brief respite on a slight decline that extends to the eighteen mile mark.

MPC: Halfway up the first hill, I came to the conclusion that looking upwards to the top of the hill was very discouraging. For all that work, you don't seem to make much headway. So I decided to keep my head down, and forge ahead on all future hills.

When I arrived at the top of the first hill, my energy was pretty much zapped. I still had two of the three Commonwealth Avenue hills to go. My mind began to lean further towards quitting than continuing. I had been on the course for over three hours, which was accomplishment for me—my previous best was 2:48 that covered 17.5 miles. My mind began saying, "You've already surpassed your best efforts. There's no disgrace in stopping. Look how many competitors are walking, or are sitting on the side of the road. There is no way they can feel worse than I do." But my heart kept saying, "Who cares how far or how long you've run if it isn't 26.2 miles?" So I continued on.

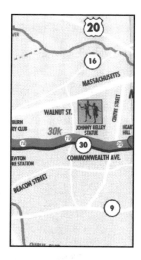

MILE NINETEEN

To elaborate upon the stature of the three hills on Commonwealth Avenue with descriptive prose would still not give this segment of the race its due. Instead, the truth of the hills' magic can only be described by the feet of the beholders:

Four-time winner Bill Rodgers: "This is the most significant stretch of course in the road racing world. The Fukuoka {Japan} route has its spots and other races have nice scenery, but there is no section that identifies the challenge and beauty of marathoning more than this section of the Boston Marathon."

John Kelley, who conquered these hills sixty times: "Those hills have special meaning to me. I have great respect for them. They've caused me a lot of problems."

Writer Jerry Nason: "These hills separates the men from the boys."

*In 1933, the **Boston Globe** described this section as the "teasing Newton Hills."*

*In 1952, the **Boston Globe** described the Commonwealth Avenue hills as a "topographical booby trap."*

*In 1965, the **Boston Globe** further described the hills as, "topographically terrorizing."*

Geoff Smith: "The hills are mountains by the time you hit them."

Ibrahim Hussein:"I will sacrifice myself on the hills."

Jean Driscoll:"The marathon is won and lost on the hills. Those who fear the hills will falter while those who attack the hills can win."

Canadian runner, Ken Parker: "It's like meeting the Queen."

Dick Hoyt, of Team Hoyt: "The hills are simply physically challenging. After almost twenty miles, the chair starts to push back on hills, causing me to exert even further energy."

Sara Mae Berman:"It's at this point that your physical effort becomes more of a mental effort. You have to want to keep going."

Uta Pippig:"The first time that runners run the race they are sometimes confused with how many hills there are on Commonwealth Avenue. But after you run the race once, you'll always remember that there are three *hills."*

At this point, the runners continue to assess their bodies and adjust their estimated time of arrival at the finish line. The lies runners told themselves back in the flats of Framingham are being introduced to the truth in the hills of Newton.

Uta Pippig:"I always reserve some extra energy for the hills. I know back in Framingham and Wellesley that they are up ahead, so I plan accordingly. While running them, I stay within my game plan unless I'm running with someone that I am unfamiliar with. Then I will try to push myself and test my competitor. If they are faster, they can go ahead. If I'm faster then I'll go ahead."

1909. Motorcycler George Proctor of Waltham broke a sprocket on his bike that sent him crashing into a family of marathon watchers. Two children were taken to the hospital and later released with minor injuries.

❧ ❧ ❧ ❧ ❧

1947. Yun Bok Suh of Korea was running in the lead when a fox terrier ran onto the course and tripped Suh to the ground. Suh, who was bloodied by the fall, seemed to get an adrenaline rush from the incident. He got to his feet and took off for the finish line and victory.

❧ ❧ ❧ ❧ ❧

1980. Runner John David Knows was knocked to his knees by a well-meaning fan who was spraying the overheated runners with his garden hose. Knows remained on the ground searching in vain for his discharged contact lenses.

The first hill has been conquered but there are still two to go. The course levels off and then declines, as does the runner's pulse. The mile zigzags through a residential neighborhood, snaking left and right. It continues past a set of traffic lights at the Chestnut Street intersection and onward to the Newton Cemetery that lies on the right halfway through the mile. Across the street from the cemetery is Wauwnet Road. The Wauwnet Road/Commonwealth Avenue corner, a quarter mile from the town hall, marks the site of the old Wauwnet Dairy Farm. In the days of the great Depression, 500 Jersey cows stopped their grazing to cheer on Clarence DeMar as he ran past.

After the Newton Cemetery, the runners move down a knoll to the Newton Town Hall which was built during the Depression.

John "Younger" Kelley used to make a point of not looking at his watch, fearing that the time he read would not be consistent with his wishes. So as he came upon the Town Hall in Newton, he would be disappointed to find that the clock on the steeple would inevitably come into his line of sight, showing the big hand five minutes faster than he had hoped.

On the left at the Town Hall, there is a quaint little walkway which is honored by the presence of a statue by Rich Munroe. It portrays two runners holding hands as they run up Heartbreak Hill. One runner recognizes the young John "Elder" Kelley who won the race in 1935. The other runner depicts an older John "Elder" Kelley who competed in the race in 1992.

MPC: During training runs with Rad, Richie and Jack Radley, we shared the duty of buying fluids, pretzels and oranges. For some reason, we always stopped at the statue of the young and old John "Elder" Kelley in order to leave a jug of water or jar of Gatorade. While driving in the car, it seemed relevant. But after running fifteen miles, it was discouraging to be reminded that Kelley was 50 years older than we were, yet we were the ones who felt like the octogenarians.

At this point of the race, there is no such thing as an easy mile. Just lifting and dropping your foot is an adventure. The aroma of cookouts is starting to affect me adversely. My left leg continues to bother me, almost giving way once.

Running past the town hall and through the Walnut Street intersection, the runner can see the second hill just past the Mile 19 signpost.

Coaxed on by her friends, Jane Weinbaum entered the 1963 race at the Centre Street intersection in Newton and went on to become the first woman ever to cross the finish line in Boston.
Photo courtesy of Boston Public Library Print Dept.

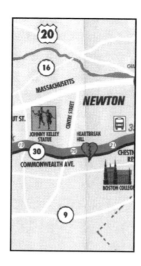

MILE TWENTY

Mile Twenty hosts the second of the three Commonwealth Avenue hills. Just past Walnut Street and the Mile Nineteen mark, the hill moves up and to the right. The uphill run lasts for about 600 and 800 yards, decent yardage for an NFL running back, but for a marathoner 20 miles into a race, the hill seems to be from here to eternity.

MPC: No mile on the course exemplifies the physical and mental challenge of the Boston Marathon more than Mile Twenty.

During a training run in February which started at the 6.5 mile mark, I was forced to stop running on the second hill because of dehydration. Desperate to find fluids, I resorted to reaching deep into the two feet of snow and started to eat vocifourously. This solved the dehydration problem, but my mind was still mush.

Distraught, because my dream of running the Boston Marathon seemed to be over, I walked a mile to a convenience store across from Boston College and started to feast on pretzels. I later wondered how I must have appeared to the other patrons at the store—snow plastered around the perimeter of my face, a runny nose, and the look of a serial killer.

The second hill ends towards the half-mile mark. The now level road continues to serpentine back and forth all the way to the Centre Street intersection where it straightens out. The residential neighborhood at this point turns into a small commercial district. On the right, at the Centre Street intersection, is the Ski & Tennis Chalet. Tom Foran, two-time third place finisher of the men's wheelchair competition, looks for a black store sign on the front of the Ski & Tennis Chalet to remind him that he has one hill to go.

Store owner Lyle Shelly lives for the Boston Marathon. Nicely situated right before the twenty mile mark, Shelly takes out his six-foot ladder from the store and perches high above the six and seven deep rows of spectators, for a wonderful vantage point to take in the race.

1985 was the year that Geoff Smith set out to break a world record. He completed his first mile in 4:31 and the first three in under fourteen minutes. He was not out to just break the record—he was out to abuse it.

Smith learned how to run like the wind as a fireman in Liverpool, England. During civil service training, the brigade was asked to run in order to keep their ladder-climbing legs in shape. The privates ran through the Liverpool fog, knowing their commanders awaited them at the finish line, which happened to be a local pub. Geoff figured out that running faster than the others would net him a well-deserved beer as he waited for his slower, less thirsty comrades. Geoff had found purpose in his runs, and a star was born.

From the soccer fields and fire poles of England to Providence College and ultimately the streets of Boston, Smith is one of the few runners ever to run a sub 4:00 minute mile, sub 1:02 half marathon and a sub 2:10 marathon.

"I'm a dinosaur in track and field events." He says, "I used to compete in thirty, forty races a year at all different distances. These days, runners like Cosmas Ndeti run two, maybe three marathons a year, and that is it. Marathoning is a career. People like myself, Alberto Salazar and others used to run the marathon as part of the normal rotation of events. It wasn't unusual for a me to run a five or ten kilometer race and then weeks later run the marathon. These days it's unheard of."

When Geoff showed up in Hopkinton, he came with the attitude "I'm going to go for it." After finishing the first half, he was on pace to break 2:06. As he ran the

1905. Fred Lorz had to jump past a horse and two bikers in the twentieth mile in order to continue on his way to the championship.

❧❧❧❧❧

1906. The *Boston Globe* reported that Newton police were tackling interlopers like Yale football players.

❧❧❧❧❧

1907. Media and fans expected Thomas Longboat to "fag out" on the hills of Newton. He didn't fag out and went on to win the race.

❧❧❧❧❧

1950. Leader Ki Yong Ham ran past the Centre Street intersection and off the course on the left side of the barricades. Police eventually directed him back to the course and onto victory.

❧❧❧❧❧

1978. As Kevin Donahue from Silver Springs, Maryland slowed to a walk up the second hill, an old man stepped out of the crowd, patted him on the back and said, "Come on son, this is the Boston Marathon."

Running on a world record pace in 1985, Geoff Smith screams in pain as his hamstrings and his record pace both cramped. Photo courtesy of Victah Sailer/McManus.

twentieth mile, he was still on a pace to break the world record when the course reared its ugly head. For a hundred years, the Marathon has had a way of humbling even the great runners, and this year was no different.

Suddenly feeling as if he'd been shot in the leg, Geoff Smith grabbed for his hamstring. On a world record pace, he was forced to come to a complete halt and look to the skies for divine intervention. Starting up again, it took him six minutes and 17 seconds to get through mile twenty. His dream of adding his name to the record book was crushed. He went on to win his second straight Boston Marathon by a margin in excess of five minutes between himself (2:14:05) and the second place finisher, Gary Tuttle (2:19:11).

"I thought it was all over," he remembers. "With the pain biting at my hamstrings, I didn't think I could take another step. But the cramp let up somewhat and I was able to run slowly and cautiously to the finish line."

As Geoff Smith walked across the finish line, many involved with the race saw this as symbolic. The quality of the field had dropped in the recent years as world class runners were migrating to races that made it worth their while. Smith's sad but victorious saunter allowed critics to point to the fact that while the winner walked across the finish line, he still beat his nearest competitor by five minutes.

In retrospect, Smith's 1985 run embodied the essence of the Boston Marathon. There was no prize money, no cars, no hidden purse—just a medal and a laurel wreath. Smith already had won the year before. He could have walked off the course in Newton and still had his name in the circle of champions. But he fought the pain and anguish because his heart told him to.

So as Geoff Smith walked across the finish line, his run evoked pathos but not pity. He had taken the Marathon course's best punch and was still standing.

1963. At the Centre Street intersection, Newton South High School student Jane Weinbaum, jumped into the race on a bet with her friends. She ran the final six miles, making her the first woman ever to run across the finish line.

❧❧❧❧❧

1978. In the past, 1972 Olympic Gold Medalist Frank Shorter had degraded the Boston course by referring to the route as illegal because of the simplicity of the down hills.

In 1978, when he finally ran Boston, the course reaped its revenge by chewing up and spitting out the condescending marathoner with a time of 2:18:15, which was beaten by twenty-two other runners.

❧❧❧❧❧

1987. Geoff Smith was again in the hunt for the championship. He had fought hard in the last miles to catch the leader Toshihiko Seko. Pulling up alongside Seko, he gave him a big smile. Seko turned away and ran on to victory. Smith, the eventual third place finisher said later, "I guess I shouldn't have smiled at him."

As 1976 winner Jack Fultz gets cooled down, the author's grandmother, Catherine Connelly (in white dress), cheers him on. Photo by Dick Raphael/*Sports Illustrated.*

With Heartbreak Hill in sight, and running gloves still in place, the author tries to put on a good face as he approaches his wife, son, and friends who were patiently waiting at the 20-mile mark.
Photo courtesy of Noreen Connelly.

Somewhere high above, the late great champions William Kennedy and Clarence DeMar must have been smiling as Smith broke the tape.

Commonwealth Avenue was built in 1895 by the Newton Boulevard Syndicate. The trolley was added the following year. This mode of transportation became popular with the affluent Bostonians interested in taking the five cent ride out to the country. The local Stanley Brothers preferred their own form of transportation, racing the Stanley Steamer up and down the road, defiantly exceeding the speed limit.

On the flat area near the end of the mile, the runners pass the Newton Tennis and Squash Club on their right. When the manager of the club was asked if the club did anything special for the race, he answered, in his most refined British voice, "Only the Squash courts are available for the members at that time of the year."

MPC: In my opinion, the second hill on Commonwealth Avenue is the toughest of the three. The first hill is attacked with great zest after making the turn at the fire station onto Commonwealth Avenue. Running Heartbreak Hill, the third hill, is a battle within the war. Runners are so geared to run the famous obstacle that the flow of adrenaline can take them over the summit. The second hill just seems to hurt more than the others.

As I struggled up the second hill, I was shocked to see how many runners were walking. The number was so extensive that at one point, a volunteer yelled out, "I only see one person running—lets go!" Luckily, I was that one person.

As I finished the second hill and approached the three-quarter mark of the mile, I was overcome with emotion. It was here where I used to stand as a young boy with my grandmother, Nana Connelly, and my two brothers and three sisters. Nana died in 1984 having fulfilled her responsibility as a Bostonian by passing on the Boston Marathon tradition from one generation to another.

My eyes filled with tears as I passed that spot. Two hundred yards up the street, past the Centre Street intersection, my wife would be waiting with friends at a house party with yet another generation of Connellys—my son Ryan.

As I approached them, I was confused. I didn't know what I wanted to do. Should I quit after completing twenty miles, running non-stop for over three hours and fifteen minutes and assuring myself a ride home? Or should I keep going. My head said stop, but my brain impulses did not make their way to the nerve endings in my legs so I just kept running.

On the sidewalk, my wife stopped to take pictures and then ran along the side of the road to wish me well. The sad thing was that she was running faster than I was.

Runners are forced to negotiate both Heartbreak Hill and the upclose-and-personal crowd.
Photo courtesy of Boston Athletic Association.

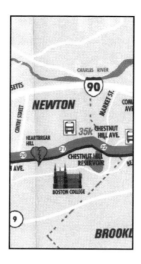

MILE TWENTY-ONE

Rob de Castella: "The race is broken down into two halves. The first half of the race is the first twenty miles. The second half of the race is the last six miles."

Some run, some walk, some crawl and some surrender, but without doubt all who pass do so with respect.

During the race's infancy, *Boston Globe* writer Lawrence Sweeney described the hills in Newton as "heartbreaking hills." As the years went by, and the hills captured more prisoners, the newest literary link to the race, Jerry Nason, formally christened the most treacherous of the three hills (because of the cumulative effect), with the befitting name of Heartbreak Hill.

The 21st mile has a flat beginning and then quickly scales upward until the runners get a break of 15 yards at the intersection of Grant Street. After that brief shift in muscle concentration, the runners are again faced with a concrete monster.

MPC: As I left my family and a ride behind, I came to the foot of Heartbreak Hill. Here, a spectator was pounding a huge base drum again and again and again. As the sound of the drum seemed to mimic my heartbeat, I felt like an Indian warrior being sent off to war.

From mile to mile, town to town, the crowd gradually turned into a mob. On Heartbreak Hill, spectators five, six, ten deep rally to this section to see men and women rage their own personal battle. Each step is an obstacle and an accomplishment. One writer likened the crowd to "the sadistic mass at the Indianapolis 500 who are more interested in human wreckage than the sporting event itself." Another writer declared: "The fans at this vantage point are sadists, flog artists and bunion mongers."

Above: At the base of Heartbreak Hill, the runners are inspired by the primal beats of an enthusiastic well-wisher in 1996. *Below:* A passionate spectator congratulates a runner after cresting Heartbreak Hill during the 100th running. Photos courtesy of FayFoto.

1975. As leader Bill Rodgers ran up the base of Heartbreak Hill, he stopped and kneeled down for more than ten seconds in order to tie his sneaker. This was one of five times that Rodgers stopped on his way to an American and Boston Marathon course record of 2:09:55.

1991. Fired John Hancock Financial Services employees threatened to picket across Heartbreak Hill. The protest was eventually canceled and the race was spared an ugly scene.

❧❧❧❧❧❧

1978. After conquering Heartbreak Hill, runner Donald Hawley was disoriented. He later said, "I didn't know where I was. I could only see little white spots in front of me."

1979. For the last two decades, runners have been greeted at the top of Heartbreak Hill by Lt. Feeley of the Newton police, who makes good use of his loud speaker to proclaim, "Congratulations! You have just conquered Heartbreak Hill!"

❧❧❧❧❧❧

1923. In hot pursuit of Clarence DeMar, Frank Zuna was brought to a stop in Mile 21 by a traffic jam of motor cars. The time Zuna lost negotiating the congestion foiled any hopes of catching the great DeMar for the victory.

For three-to-four tenths of a mile, each competitor takes a step closer to the peak of Heartbreak Hill and the finish line. Finally, the runners approach the promised land. To the spectators, it seems like arms and legs have done all the work, but in actuality the competitors relied mainly on one muscle—the heart.

At the top, the scene is a picture of elation—crowds salute the runners for their effort, runners throw gloves and hats to the crowd in appreciation of their support.

Halfway through the mile, at the top of the hill, the road drops to the right before rising cruelly for one last brief but painful moment.

Dick O'Brien, a citizen of Newton, lives at the peak of Heartbreak Hill. Each year, he celebrates Marathon Day with a cookout for his family and friends. Dick usually misses the race because he has to man the barbecue grill, but one year he let the burgers burn so he could see his oldest son run the race.

"When my son approached, it looked as if he was near death. As he passed in front of the house, the only thing he could think about was stopping and going to bed. But the crowd wouldn't let him. Like a supernatural act, the crowd lifted him over the hill with their screams of support."

The eldest O'Brien child went on to finish the race. Afterwards, he described his feat like a true Bostonian. "It was like hitting a baseball over the Green Monster at Fenway Park."

By the way, now that they have placed some portable bathrooms at the top of Heartbreak Hill, the O'Briens don't need to hire a guard for their front door anymore.

The end of the mile moves right and downhill past the front gate of Boston College.

The Gothic steeples of Boston College stand guard over the 21-mile mark. Photo courtesy of FayFoto.

Founded by Jesuit Priests in 1863, Boston College charged less than $100 in tuition costs and $1 for the library and athletic fee, to 450 male students in 1897. Now it costs almost 15,000 young men and women $26,086 to live and learn at B.C.

Doug Flutie (football star), Ed McMahon (Tonight Show and Star Search) and the late Tip O'Neal (Speaker of the House) were some of the school's famous graduates. The most heralded faculty member is Raymond McNally, who also happens to be the country's foremost expert on Count Dracula.

The downhill past the school has been infamous for testing spent quads, and for teaching elated runners that they have five more miles to go.

Women's runner Kathleen Beebee, who has finished in the top 40 twice and placed third in the women's 50-59 yr.

old class in 1996 with a time of 3:16:47, recalled what she would like to be her most forgettable trip down this challenging hill. "I had just reached the top of Heartbreak Hill and I felt terrible. I knew that I had to finish if I had come this far. So, as I ran down the back side of Heartbreak Hill, I took a peek at the John Hancock skyscraper which sat in the sky six miles away. I noticed that it was swaying back and forth. This was not a good sign. But being a stubborn Irish woman from County Mayo, I worked my way into Boston to the turn onto Hereford Street. My friends there said that I looked deathly gray. I collapsed to the ground with the finish line in sight. I was taken by ambulance to the nearest hospital where I recovered physically but it took me a year to recover from the depression caused by the agony of falling so close to the finish line."

Kathleen Beebee went on to run other marathons and the Hancock has since stopped swaying. But her experience was a reminder to all runners. There is more to the Boston Marathon than conquering Heartbreak Hill.

MPC: As I struggled up Heartbreak Hill, it didn't seem any harder than the steps on level ground. Every time I put my foot down was a painful experience.

Halfway up the hill, a woman spectator lost sight of her baby who had run out onto the middle of the course. In an effort to sidestep the child, I had to alter my running pattern. This one change caused me great discomfort.

Continuing up the hill, I was able to pick up my head enough to see an older runner working it hard. Looking further, I noticed that the man had a prosthesis on one of his legs. His efforts inspired me and made me proud to be part of an event where courage is just as important as athletic ability. When I watched highlights of the race on the news later that day, I caught sight of this same man crossing the finish line. His success made a powerful statement about the will of someone who won't be denied.

As I reached the peak, the crowd was going crazy. I decided to move to the side and join the party after beating Heartbreak Hill. It was at that moment that I realized the crowd had been drinking for over four hours. An enthusiastic student almost knocked me back into mile 15 as he reached back, and crashed his hand into mine an in effort to congratulate me with a high-five.

The true enjoyment of conquering Heartbreak Hill comes later when you replay the race in your mind or discuss the feeling with fellow marathoners.

After leaving the merry group at the top of Heartbreak Hill, I started to descend. Outside the Boston College gates, my brother Kevin was waiting with our friends Tim and Mary Kate. They were both past survivors of the race. Tim and Mary Kate wished me well while Kevin joined me for the final five miles. As we took off, I was hoping he would say, "You look terrible. You have to stop." But instead he said, "You look great. Let's do it!"

John "Younger" Kelley runs with the 1959 lead past St. Ignatius Church which stands on the Boston College Campus. Photo courtesy of Boston Athletic Association.

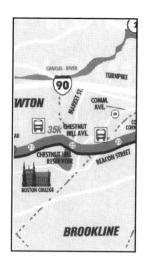

MILE TWENTY-TWO

The hills are done, but the race goes on. Runners must be careful not to let their guard down too early. There are still more than five miles to go.

MPC: During the months of preparation before the race, beginners like Rad, Richie, Jackie and myself came up with a number of theories in an attempt to convince ourselves that we had the capacity to run the Boston Marathon. One of the theories we formulated was that if we made it over Heartbreak Hill then the rest of the race was smooth sailing. It was anything but.

Two-time winner John "Elder" Kelley had fought through the hills in an effort to catch the 1936 leader "Tarzan" Brown. In Mile Twenty-two, Kelley finally caught the fading leader. As he passed Brown, Kelley made the mistake of tapping Brown on the shoulder and saying, "Nice try kid, I'll take it from here."

Spurred on by this swashbuckling maneuver, Brown dug down deep and did the improbable. He regained the lead and held on to win leaving Kelley to eat humble pie.

*Brown, a Native American from the Narragansett tribe of Rhode Island, had finished 13th the year before. In crossing the finish line that year, he caught the attention of the media because he was running barefoot. This year he not only raised the eyebrows of the media but also their politically incorrect pens. The following day the **Boston Globe** reported, "Brown ran the panting palefaces into the ground with a modern day tomahawk of a 'killer' pace." They continued, "Many Indians cheered on their blood brother. They must have been notified by smoke telegraph."*

His mother told him, "They're making fun of you. Show them." In 1939, Brown showed them again by winning his second marathon, although it didn't curb the poison pen of reporters: "The indomitable Narragansett brave whooped more powerfully then his warlike ancestors."

Even though the Boston Marathon and society have evolved and matured over the years, it is hard to believe that stories like the above, and headlines such as "Atomic Boy," in reference to 1951 winner Shigeki Tanaka who was from Hiroshima and "Jap wins" (1953) could have been socially acceptable.

The runners move past Boston College in a continuous descent of almost a half mile. At this point, runners must assess their energy reserves and glycogen stores in order to determine if they can push themselves or if they should hold on for dear life. Those who are holding on realize that their split times, which looked so good back in Natick and Framingham, are now out the window and that survival is their only goal.

This type of downshifting and upshifting, similar to the Newton Lower Falls section at the 16-mile mark, plays havoc with the runners' legs. Sometimes the downhill that stretches from the peak of Heartbreak Hill past Boston College and down to the Lake Street intersection claims as many runners as the hills that precede this descent.

Past champion, Rob de Castella called this section of the race "an anatomical challenge."

Two-time champion, Johnny Kelley called it the "haunted mile." Because of the upcoming cemetery on the right, Jerry Nason called it "the graveyard for champions." Olympic Silver medalist, John Treacy noted, "The great mystique of Heartbreak Hill is not getting up it. It's getting down it."

Three-time winner Cosmas Ndeti observed, "The race doesn't begin until the 35 kilometer mark [halfway

1903. Sammy Mellor, running with the lead, slowed to a walk after battling the hills and became the first leader to fall victim to the haunted mile. He eventually finished in second place with a time of 2:47:13, almost six minutes behind John Lorden's 2:41:29.

1911. Festus Madden had relinquished the lead several miles back but was still in hot pursuit of the leader Clarence DeMar when he was hit by a car. Temporarily slowed down by the minor collision, he ended up finishing second.

1922. Leader James Henigan's legs began to tighten as he made his way down the hill at Boston College. Approaching the Lake Street intersection, his worsening legs forced him to stop. In an effort to restart his engine, Henigan grabbed a yard stick from a fan and beat it against his legs—with few results other than red welts. Henigan was forced to drop out of the race while Clarence DeMar raced on to victory.

1923. Albert Michelson, a one-time leader of the race, had struggled for the past two miles. As he approached Lake Street, he stopped. Michelson's attendant, who had ridden next to him on a bike throughout the race, gave him a flask with peppermint water and a pill of "unknown purpose," reported the Boston Globe. These seemed to rejuvenate him, and he finished fourth.

1938. Olympian Stylianos Kyriakides from Greece pulled out of the race because of blisters just before the Lake Street intersection. He proceeded to jump on the train at the Boston College Station and eventually found his way to Boston.

❧ ❧ ❧ ❧ ❧ ❧

1942. As Governor Maurice Tobin attempted to assist his favorite runner, Fred McGlone, he slammed the door of his car on his hand after providing water to the fading pre-race favorite.

❧ ❧ ❧ ❧ ❧ ❧

1947. Runner Michael Kish was hit by a car and sent sprawling onto the sidewalk by Boston College. After receiving medical care for his bleeding head and arms, he continued on to finish the race.

❧ ❧ ❧ ❧ ❧ ❧

1972. Leaders Olavi Suomalainen and Jacinto Sabinal were almost run over by the press bus just after passing the college. In an effort to brace themselves, they held on to each other to keep from being crushed.

through mile 22]." In 1993 he was 16th at the bottom of Heartbreak Hill, third when he crested the peak and went on from here to victory. In 1995, he didn't take the lead till the 35km mark and at that point he never looked back.

At the bottom of the hill, after Boston College, the route passes St. Ignatius Church on the right and the Boston College Green Line Trolley Station on the left. The road now becomes a four-lane thruway divided down the middle by the train tracks for the Green Line "B" train. Runners stay to the right of the road.

An eighth of a mile further, the field moves past the Lake Street intersection and up a slight incline with St. John's Seminary and the Cardinal's home on the left and Evergreen Cemetery on the right. The road inclines slightly again and the runners are now sandwiched by student-occupied apartment buildings which line both sides of the street. Ahead at the end of the mile, the Chestnut Hill Reservoir hugs the right side of the course up to Chestnut Hill Street where the runners turn and temporarily leave Commonwealth Avenue.

In 1901, Ronald MacDonald—local hero, past champion and Boston College student—was running with the leaders past the Chestnut Hill Reservoir when he took ill. He was handed something from the crowd and moments later dropped to the ground and out of the race. Some witnesses claimed that a certain Dr. Thompson had given him stimulants that had an effect other than the one intended. Dr. Thompson disputed this account and claimed someone had handed MacDonald a sponge saturated with chloroform. Thompson felt it was intentional, "It couldn't well have been an accident," Thompson said, "when there was so much money up on the race."

MacDonald claimed a soldier, who he was assigned

to assist him, had handed him a sponge that had been soaked by the contents of a mysterious canteen. Upon sucking the sponge dry, he collapsed to the ground, his throat burning from the unknown fluid. In an effort to save him, Dr. Thompson provided two strychnine pills that MacDonald claims saved his life. Upon hearing this explanation, Henry Holton of the BAA called this story, "An excuse of a crybaby who was trying to cover up the disgrace of letting down the number of American bettors who had put their trust in him."

*A recent investigation by **Boston College Magazine**, examined the controversy, raising more questions than answers. The mystery has never been solved.*

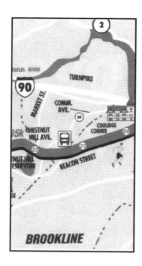

MILE TWENTY-THREE

At the beginning of Mile Twenty-Three, the runners are treated to a downhill that would be rated a Black Diamond slope if this were a ski resort. After a right turn from Commonwealth onto Chestnut Hill Street the runners descend 80 feet closer to sea level as they move past a public pool and skating rink on their right and the former location of the Bill Rodgers Running Center on their left.

Uta Pippig: "I look forward to the right turn which moves you towards Cleveland Circle. If you let yourself go just a little bit, and don't push to hard, you can really fly."

Down the middle the trolley tracks protrude from the course (similar to Framingham) and must be negotiated with care. The tracks lead the runners down into the gauntlet of Cleveland Circle.

The Cleveland Circle five-way intersection is filled with inebriated college students, loose pavement, treacherous train tracks, and a sharp left turn on to Beacon Street at the base of the hill. All these factors makes this location golden for the spectators and a nightmare for the runners.

This is especially true for the wheelchair competitors. Working downhill at speeds close to 35 miles per hour, the runners are forced to break themselves down, navigate the raised and sometimes slippery set of tracks, and at the same time take a left turn.

The Cleveland Circle area is strictly commercial. Store owners can pay landlords upwards of $40 per square foot for the honor of running a business in this area although college students who frequent the two drinking establishments in the Circle, Maryanne's and Cityside, are more interested in the price of a Bud than the overhead cost to run a business in the Cleveland Circle district.

Running in the greatest duel in the history of the Boston Marathon, Dick Beardsley and Alberto Salazar
battle each other, the crowd, a mounted policeman and a number of police motorcycles in 1982.
Photo courtesy of Robert Mahoney.

1971. As three time winner Sara Mae Berman ran with the lead towards Cleveland Circle, the second place women's runner, Nina Kuscsik (1972 winner) passed her. After relinquishing the lead for the first time, Sara Mae said to herself, "I'm not going to let anyone beat me. Seeing her run by was like a kick in the pants. I knew that there was another level that I could push myself to and I did it."

1981. As Toshihiko Seko and Craig Virgin ran past the Bill Rodgers Running Store, Seko made his move and never looked back. At the press conference later, Seko found it ironic, that en route to breaking Rodger's course record, he had decided to make his most critical move at Rodgers' store.

1981. Woman runner Patti Catalano was sideswiped by a police horse while making her way through Cleveland Circle. Somehow she was able to keep her balance and finish the race with an American record time of 2:27:51 but finished second to New Zealander Allison Roe.

1980. Wheelchair leader George Murray caught his wheel on one of the dangerous train tracks as he attempted to cross through Cleveland Circle. He worked feverishly to free the tire, but he was unable to repair the damaged wheel in time to hold the lead and became another victim of the dangerous conditions at Cleveland Circle.

The manager at the Cityside Bar described the profits of Marathon Day: "It's blood money! With two policeman working the door and diners milking their outside table on the roof, the day can be more trouble than the money is worth." But as Mayor Mann of Newton said earlier, The Cityside has a moral obligation to quench the thirst of those parched spectators. The manager of Maryanne's (previously known as the Jungle) described the scene at his establishment as a "madhouse."

Uta Pippig, "For the first time in the race, you can feel the closeness of the finish line."

Past the Circle, the runners move to the right side of Beacon Street. This road, like the bottom of Commonwealth Avenue, is split down the middle by the Green Line train tracks. These tracks carry the C train at a very deliberate pace. A runner who throws in the towel, and jumps on the train, realizes that he/she probably would have arrived in Boston faster by running. A local writer once quipped, "A person tied to the green line tracks was found dead—he starved to death."

The route works it way straight down Beacon Street with a slight incline. This area is a mix of apartment buildings and businesses. In the mile's first quarter, the race moves into the town of Brookline.

Brookline was incorporated in 1705. In an effort to establish its own identity, residents of the "Hamlet of Muddy River" petitioned the city of Boston for the right to become their own town. After much dispute, it was finally agreed and a new town was born. The town's boundaries were set by using the line drawn by the Smelt Brook which ran through Judge Samuel Sewall's 350-acre farm. He had inherited the property from his wife who had inherited it from her father. Judge Sewall not only drew notoriety for being the owner of the land that marked the town's border with the city of Boston; he was also known for being the judge who had sentenced the Salem Witches to death in the 1600s.

The town of Brookline has an estimated population of 55,946. The town stretches over almost seven square acres.

As they continue down Beacon Street, many runners realize that their speeds have been greatly reduced when they see they are no longer gaining on competitors who are walking.

At the same time, male chauvinists are bothered by the fact that women runners are starting to pick off men runners by the dozen at this section of the race.

Vincent Chiapetta, President of the Road Running Club of America, stated that women had a superior build for running. "They are light-boned, they have stamina, a good cardio vascular history and good lung ratio."

Kathy Switzer on this experience: "When you are finishing strong, you can pick off as many as a hundred people in a very short distance. The people who are struggling seem like they are going backwards while you feel like the course is coming to you."

Up an incline and down the other side, the runners move towards the end of the mile near the Washington Street intersection. On the corner is The Hammond bar. One year, bartender and part owner Don Connors was amazed to look up from the taps to find a runner dressed as Kermit the Frog who had bypassed the water stops for a cold draft. Donny obliged and sent the runner away a satisfied Muppet.

The runners are now just a short distance from Coolidge Corner, just two miles from the finish.

1997. In the midst of her run to become the most decorated champion in Boston Marathon history, seven-time champ Jean Driscoll found herself in a head-to-head duel with Australian Louise Sauvage. As the two competitors raced down the hill into Cleveland Circle, Driscoll caught a wheel on an exposed train track, sending her to the ground with a flat tire and Sauvage onto the podium. Driscoll lost her chance for her eighth laurel wreath but paid the course its due respect after the race: "I had a great race until I met Cleveland Circle."

1976. Running with the lead, Jack Fultz entered the chaos of Cleveland Circle. As he came to the bottom of the hill, he turned left too early and started to run on the westbound side of Beacon Street. The crowd, not knowing any better, separated so he could proceed. Finally, someone in the crowd yelled at him that he was on the wrong side. Jack made a 90° turn and worked his way over the train tracks to the eastbound side and was on his way to victory.

1968. As Amby Burfoot ran through Cleveland Circle, he developed a side cramp. Fighting through the cramp, Burfoot felt he was slowing down substantially. He didn't dare look over his shoulder because he feared the entire marathon field was closing on him. Burfoot spent the greatest five miles of his life in a state of panic waiting to be passed. Finally, with yards to go to the finish line, he turned and, to his relief, didn't see anybody. He went on to win the race.

Accompanied by the Green-Line on their right, the 1996 leaders take another step toward the finish line in Boston. Photo courtesy of Victah Sailer.

1979. As leader Joan Benoit passed through Mile twenty-three, a rambunctious fan ran out onto the course. He held a beer in one hand and a Red Sox cap in the other. As he jogged along with Benoit he said, "Either wear the hat or chug the beer." She chose the hat.

৵৵৵৵৵৵

1948. Running stride for stride throughout the race, leaders Gerard Cote and Ted Vogel waged a running duel that almost turned into a street brawl. Cote, a four-time champion from Canada who was a great snowshoe racer, had spent a significant amount of energy attempting to distract Vogel from his game plan. Cote started by stepping on the back of Vogel's sneakers early in the race. On the Newton hills, Cote continuously cut in front of Vogel in an attempt to break his stride. After coming down the hills, Cote took a glass of water and tossed it over his head hitting Vogel and sending him over the edge. After passing through Cleveland Circle, Vogel ran up along Cote and offered the Canadian runner the opportunity to settle their problem in the middle of Beacon Street with the championship of the Boston Marathon on the line. Cote ignored the offer and ran on to victory.

MPC: As my brother and I ran down Beacon Street, the pain was constant. By now, I couldn't hold my head up. My brother would inform me when there was a walker up ahead. Gatorade and water would hit the back of my mouth and come right back out. The sea breeze was picking up and the temperature seemed to drop by over ten degrees. The Mylar blankets, given to runners on the course, were blowing in the wind and snapping me in the face.

Uta Pippig, "Running down Beacon Street is pretty cool. The people are so knowledgeable about the race and the sport. Many of them have radios and are aware of who is leading and are ready for the leaders as they pass."

MILE TWENTY-FOUR

With the shadows of Boston's skyscrapers drawing nearer, the runners move through Cleveland Circle, down Beacon Street and up and down the small waves of inclines and declines toward Coolidge Corner which sits on a plateau following a slight upgrade. After the runners work their way through the Corner at the intersection of Harvard and Beacon, the course moves downhill toward the end of the mile.

The Coolidge Corner area is surrounded by commercial businesses, apartments and condo-ized buildings. Commercial space can cost upwards of $35 per squre foot, apartments rent for more than $1,200 a month plus $80 a month for a parking spot, and a 1000-foot condo sells for approximately $170,000.

The diversity of everyday life in Coolidge Corner makes this area a small melting pot. Inhabitants and visitors are exposed to multiple lifestyles, religions and cultures. This is reflected in the variety of delicatessens, movie theaters, and ethnic specialty shops.

Coolidge Corner was named after a local store owner, David Sullivan Coolidge. His general store, which was named Coolidge & Bros, was located on the corner of Harvard and Beacon streets. Harvard Street was given its name because it led to the University. Beacon Street was a major thruway from the city to the country. In 1888, it was widened to 200 feet. At the same time the electric train, the longest continuous electric train route in the world, was put into operation.

The aristocrats of Brookline, who could afford their own form of transportation, had long been opponents of the train. Said one blueblood: "Unpleasant mechanism of unproven worth. Vulgar common carrier."

One wonders if those aristocrats of Coolidge Corner would have snubbed their noses at their latter day neighbor John Kennedy who introduced the world to space travel 120 years later.

Not to be outdone by the upper class, bricklayer and runner William Kennedy was applauded by his brothers-in-trade who were working on a nearby building in 1917. As Kennedy ran through Coolidge Corner on his way to victory, the bricklayers took a quick break from their toil in order to slap their bricks together in a relevant form of cheer.

Kennedy was exhorted not only for his championship run but also for his pre-race call to arms. With the war to end all wars being waged across the sea, Kennedy urged all American runners to run the race of their lives. This would prove to the whole world that Americans were superior in every branch of life. So with a handkerchief embroidered with a miniature American Flag draped across his head, Kennedy went on to win the marathon in a victory that one official called, "The greatest athletic victory of this country and of any country."

In the early years of the race, the affluent residents of Coolidge Corner sat in their windows and acknowledged the runners by waving their lacy handkerchiefs.

Throughout the history of the race, the crowds and chaotic atmosphere at Coolidge Corner, just two plus miles from the finish line, have made this a pivotal spot. At times, runners have been forced to run single file through the onslaughts of well-wishers. Police cars and other moving vehicles often become more of a hindrance than a help. Surviving Coolidge Corner is one of those battles within the war.

But in 1980, Bill Rodgers faced a danger far greater than vehicular congestion at this site.

President Jimmy Carter of the United States ordered a boycott of the 1980 Olympics, which were being held in Moscow. This was done in order to condemn the USSR's attempt to occupy Afghanistan.

Marathoner Bill Rodgers verbally protested the boy-

1898. Running through Coolidge Corner with a substantial lead, Larry Brignolia slipped on a rock and twisted his ankle. As he attempted to get up, medics held him down for five minutes to make sure he was capable of continuing the race. The delay cost Brignolia the world record and nearly cost him the race as popular Harvard runner Dick Grant closed in on Brignolia, but never passed him.

1910. A car, making its way across the route, ran over a girl causing injuries to her head and shoulders. The driver was warned and sent on his way.

1915. Leader Clifton Horne was beginning to sway back and forth as his lead faded. Attendants raced to a local store and bought two raw eggs for Horne, who reluctantly consumed them. He eventually lost the lead and finished second.

1919. At the starting line, Chicago runner, Frank Gillespie, tried on his new sneakers for the first time. On discovering that the sneakers were to tight, he cut a slit in the front of each, exposing the five toes on each foot. It helped, but not enough. Arriving at Coolidge Corner with the lead, Frank Gillespie was forced to slow down with blisters and cuts, allowing three other runners to overtake him.

1930. Clarence DeMar, the eventual winner of the '35 race, had his foot run over and his shoe ripped by a passing motor car.

1975. Ron Hill passed fellow Canadian, Jerome Drayton, who had stopped running, and was sitting by the side of course. Hill offered him some advice: "Get up and walk if you have to, but finish the damn race!"

1963. Running past Coolidge Corner, Aurel Vandendriessche from Belgium passed Ethiopian runner Abebe Bikila for good. Bikila was an international superstar after winning the 1960 Olympic marathon race in Rome in his bare feet. Four years later he repeated his Olympic victory, this time with sneakers.

1976. As leader Jack Fultz worked through the 90° heat of Beacon Street, he began to feel giddy. First he started to giggle as he realized he had an opportunity to achieve his greatest dream. Next, he found himself watching himself run from above like a sports commentator analyzing his run. The out-of-body experience is not uncommon for marathoners, but it certainly can be eerie. Finally Fultz caught himself rehearsing answers for the press conference. He later explained, "If I was going to win it [which he did], I didn't want to be full of cliches and one liners. I wanted to sound intelligent."

cott, and spoke out strongly against the President. (Rodgers had been a conscientious objector during the Vietnam War as had 1973 winner, Jon Anderson.) He also pledged to affirm his position by wearing a black armband during his run in the 1980 Boston Marathon.

In response, a crazed "patriot" called the Bill Rodgers Running Center days before the race. The caller pledged that Rodgers would never run through Coolidge Corner alive. This threat was taken seriously, but there was not much the police could do when there were more than a million people standing along a 26-mile stretch.

Rodgers ran the race, won the race and survived. He didn't wear the black arm band and moved quickly enough to avoid any would-be assassin. He had a tough time staying focused with the yelling of the boo-birds and the number of fists that were shaken in his face.

Coolidge Corner escaped the mantle of death and tragedy in 1980. But, on December 30, 1994, Coolidge Corner made national news when a pro-life zealot crashed into an abortion clinic and killed two women and wounded others in a demented attempt to prove his point.

At the end of the mile, the runners move past Coolidge Corner down a hill with the Holiday Inn on their left. Within the next 24 hours, this hotel will be fully booked for the following year's Marathon week.

In yet another attempt to stage a picket across the marathon route, Boston hotel workers threatened to protest a recent change in work benefits at the expense of the race. Tommy Leonard of the Eliot Lounge, upset by this type of demonstration, remarked that "stopping the marathon is like shooting the Easter Bunny."

Making their way down Beacon Street, friends Michael Radley and Rich Twombly move yet another step closer to the finish line. Photo courtesy of Victah Sailer.

1983. When the street crowds parted to let Greg Meyer through, he looked back towards Coolidge Corner but was unable to find his nearest competitor. "The crowd seem to open up in front of me like a snake eating, and close behind me like a snake swallowing."

⸙⸙⸙⸙⸙⸙

1990. Watching the race from her home in Georgia, 1978 winner Gayle Barron was disappointed to see the tight crowd control that has been implemented by the BAA. "Back when I won the race, the marathon was a personal event between the runners and the fans. I ran the last miles in 1978 on a route with just enough space for one runner to squeeze through. Every step had a fan, on each side, just inches from my ear yelling encouragement."

⸙⸙⸙⸙⸙⸙

MPC. By the time my brother and I made it through Coolidge Corner, it was close to 4:30 in the afternoon. I had been running for four hours and only had two and half miles to go. For the first time since the six-mile mark, I started to think that I had a chance to finish.

Although the crowd had grown smaller by this time, there were still plenty of spectators cheering us on. I wondered whether I looked as bad as I felt. Even though I couldn't pick my head up to see the many onlookers, I listened carefully for any disparaging comments that might have confirmed my misery.

From the side of the road, I heard someone yell, "Hey it's Michael Connelly—Alright!" I moved my head to the side just enough to spot Joe and Kevin Radley, the brothers of Michael and Jack. Joe held a video camera as he yelled. Although it was great to hear the big-hearted cheer it was too late in the race to affect my spirits. I wondered if the other guys had passed. I hoped so. The thought provided motivation to push on. I didn't want to be the only one of the four who didn't conquer the Boston Marathon.

With the Citgo Fuel sign in the background, runners struggle up to the last real topographical challenge of the race. Photo courtesy of FayFoto.

MILE TWENTY-FIVE

After Coolidge Corner, the runners are still escorted by the C train which runs along on their left. Halfway through Mile Twenty-five, the train goes underground, and the runners are left to their own means to find the finish line. At the spot where the train goes underground, sits O'Leary's, an Irish Pub. The owner, Aengus O'Leary, is accustomed to his steady customers throwing a cold one down and zipping out to see the leaders run by. In 1993, the pub became an impromptu refreshment stop for two priests from Ireland who were running the race. Each bellied up for some late carbo-loading, compliments of a properly poured Guinness that gave them enough fuel to get to the finish line. The owner had one thing to say about the condition of the two runners: "They were thirsty."

The twenty-fifth mile starts out downhill and then flattens out for about a quarter of the mile. With less than two miles to go in the race, the runners enter the city limits of Boston.

In 1630, Boston was founded and named after Saint Botolph, a town in Lincolnshire, England. It had been previously known by the name of Shawmut, the Native American word for "living waters." The city was formerly dominated by three hills with water on three sides. The hills were eventually scaled down and used as landfill to make the Back Bay and Copley Square out of the Charles River marsh.

Over the years Boston has been the sight of such time-honored events as the Boston Massacre, the Boston Tea Party and the Battle of Bunker Hill.

During the early 1800s, Boston was a mecca for the abolitionist movement. Many runaway slaves worked their way to Boston where they found refuge. The first all black-regiment, the 54th, came from Boston and fought valiantly during the Civil War. Much later, Boston became known as the home of the television show and drinking establishment known as Cheers, actually the real life Bull and Finch.

Boston has always been known for its prominent citizens and affluent families including Benjamin Franklin, Samuel Adams, the Cabots, Lodges and Saltonstalls, all of whom figured in the molding of this international city.

Currently, Boston has a population of almost 600,000 people across an area of ninety square acres. The present mayor of Boston, Tom Menino, looks forward each year to the running of the Boston Marathon. "No tradition quite captures the spirit of Boston like the Boston Marathon. Boston is a world class city, yet it's also a city of neighborhoods. As runners from all over the world run through the city's streets, spectators from all over rally together to welcome them and spur them on. It's incredible to me how, year after year, the Boston Marathon brings people together like that. The crowds aren't rooting for anyone in particular—they're rooting for everyone. Because on marathon day, everyone is a Bostonian!"

The runners move through an open intersection at Park and Beacon Streets only to confront the unexpected obstacle of Citgo Hill.

In 1996, thirty-year old Uta Pippig of Germany chose this spot to record one of the great comebacks and courageous victories in the history of the race. Battling diarrhea and menstrual bleeding, Pippig was chasing after Tegla Loroupe from Kenya. As she closed in on the front runner, Pippig ran to the side of the road and grabbed a water bottle. She then returned to the middle of the route, ripped the top of the container off with her teeth, slugged the water, spiked the bottle down on the ground and then proceeded to pass Loroupe for good and was on her way to her third straight Boston Marathon victory.

Uta Pippig remembers it vividly. "Four different times during the race, the pain was so bad that I contemplated dropping out of the race all together. Somehow I kept going and pushing myself. As I approached Citgo Hill, I saw Tegla up ahead and I said to myself, 'Come on Uta this is your chance.' Somehow I caught her. I don't know how I did it. I replay that part of the race in my mind and I still can't explain how I did it. I guess I won't figure it out until I run the race again and pass that spot. In retrospect I would say this was my greatest victory with respect to overcoming mental and physical adversity. Usually there is a plateau of pain that you can push past, but this day presented more than I ever imagined."

This unpleasant bump in the course captured its name from the large neon sign, advertising Citgo Fuel that is situated high in Kenmore Square. The Citgo sign has dominated Kenmore Square and the Green Wall at nearby Fenway Park since 1965. In the early 1970s, it was shut down because of the energy crisis. But it was soon revived, and was eventually listed as a potential historical landmark.

Citgo Hill comes at a bad time on the course and has a surprisingly negative affect upon the athlete. At this point, the runners' systems are beginning to shut down. Peripheral vision is reduced to about two yards on either side, and the runner's range of hearing is greatly impaired. Some runners feel as though they are undergoing an out-of-body experience, and in a way, they might want it to be.

Three-time winner Sara Mae Berman: "Citgo Hill feels like Mt. Washington. When you get to the base of the hill and look up, your body tells you that it doesn't want to go."

1984/1985 winner Geoff Smith: "In 1984, I didn't even know it was there. I felt great at the time, and just breezed over it. In 1985, when I struggled to make it to the finish line with cramps, I was shocked to find this hill in the middle of mile 25. I wondered if it was always there, or if it was new."

MPC: Citgo Hill, like Heartbreak Hill, wasn't any less difficult than any other step on the course. As we made it to the twenty-five mile mark, I was surprised that my thoughts turned negative. Instead of thinking, "just one mile to go," I was consumed with the thought that one more mile represented four trips around my high school football field—a distance I had trouble with just seven months before this race.

Halfway over the uphill bridge which runs over train tracks and the Mass Turnpike, the runners pass into the last full mile of the race. Those who have survived this far begin to curse King Edward VII of England, who ordered the distance of the race to be increased from twenty-five miles to twenty-six miles three hundred and eighty five yards for the 1908 Olympics.

Morrison

Jas Henigan

Leading Boston aa marathon 192

led for 16 miles

James Henigan, the 1931 winner, is surrounded by the entourage which always encircles the leader.
Photo courtesy of the *Boston Herald*.

MILE TWENTY-SIX

As the runners descend into Kenmore Square, Beacon Street delivers the runners back onto Commonwealth Avenue (home of the hills). The route continues on a level grade through the end of Kenmore Square.

Kenmore Square has long been compared to Times Square in New York because of the intersecting streets (Beacon, Commonwealth and Brookline) and the unique angle that they adjoin. Like Times Square, this location is ideal for billboard advertisements.

Kenmore Square, best known for its close proximity to Fenway Park and the Boston Red Sox, is also a bustling gathering spot for the thousands of downtown college students from Boston University and the colleges of Simmons, Emmanuel and Wheelock. The Square adopted its name from the Green Line train stop which is set in the middle of this chaotic Boston cornerstone. It was once known as Governor Square and was the center of Boston's hotel district. Hotels such as the Somerset, Braemore, Sheraton, Buckminster and Kenmore all stood here, only to give way to condominiums, nightclubs and Boston University dormitories.

Filled with students lugging schoolbooks, girls with purple hair and commuters hustling to and from the public transportation, Kenmore Square is a distinctive segment of both Boston and the Marathon.

Bars in Kenmore Square, like bars all along the route, take advantage of Marathon Day to attract customers. The Rath Skeller hires a band called the Bristols that is comprised of beautiful young girls. "They can play, too," says the manager.

Another bar in the square hangs a sign "Rosie Ruiz Started Here" in honor of the woman "runner" from New York who jumped into the race at Kenmore Square and went on to set the third fastest time in the history of the race.

The square is also the place where 35,000 Red Sox fans empty out from the 11:00 A.M. game in time to see the leaders rip by. One year, several Red Sox players scurried out of their locker room in full uniform in order to admire their fellow athletes.

In earlier days, the now long-departed Boston Braves and the Boston Red Sox used to take turns hosting double-headers on Marathon Day. The first game was played in the morning, followed by a break between games so that fans and players could see the race. The second game was played later in the afternoon.

The route moves the runners down from Coolidge Corner, over the Citgo hill and dropping through Kenmore Square which is just a mile from the finish line. Years ago, the runners would began to saliva as they could almost smell the beef stew that was served at the finish line when the number of runners was more manageable. At this point in the race the runners are less concerned with food and more interested in crossing the finish line.

*Food was certainly the last thing on John Kelley's mind when he entered Kenmore Square in 1935 with a 500-yard lead over Pat Dengis. Kelley, who had been gobbling chocolate glucose pills along the route, had struggled with his stomach ever since Coolidge Corner. When he arrived at Kenmore Square, his stomach woes forced him to come to an abrupt halt, so abrupt that the press car behind him almost flattened him. While Kelley bent over, at the waist, in an attempt to conquer the pain, the crowd urged the hometown favorite to proceed. He did, for a couple feet, until he stopped again. At this point, the crowd went into a frenzy. Pat Dengis was closing the gap and Kelley had to move or lose. According to the following day's **Boston Globe**, Kelley applied the "Roman Cure." Sticking his fingers down his throat he relieved himself of his discomfort and was off on his way to win the first of his two Boston Marathon championships. Kelley later said, "I overdosed on glucose pills."*

1931. As local favorite Jim Henigan ran through mile twenty-five, his oldest son saw him and reported to other family members, "Pa's in front, but gosh he's going awfully slow."

Due to Henigan's deteriorating appearance, a fan showered him with cold water from a milk bottle as he walked through Kenmore Square. The press bus, which usually sped ahead of the runners to the finish line, decided to remain with the leader in hope of capturing his inevitable collapse. Henigan, who had dropped out of his first seven races, eventually made his way to the finish line to break the tape and ruin the hopes of the sadistic camera crew.

1936. A physically spent and mentally exhausted "Tarzan" Brown entered Kenmore Square with the lead. As he attempted to move through the square, he swerved left and right, almost drunk-like and was almost hit by a passing car. Brown somehow regained enough strength to finish for the championship.

1981. Coming down the other side of Citgo Hill, Pat Holly became victim to the chaotic conditions in Kenmore Square when his wheelchair flipped after hitting a raised manhole cover. This mishap cost Holly a broken shoulder and a finish at Boston.

1981. Craig Virgin, a world class marathoner, described the run through Kenmore Square: "The crowd can suffocate you here, and make you become claustrophobic."

1961. John "Younger" Kelley continued his stretch of frustrating runs when he was passed at Charlesgate West by three-time winner Eino Oksanen. In his career, Kelley finished second five times and in the top ten, ten times. He won in 1957, becoming the only runner from the Boston Athletic Association ever to win the Boston Marathon.

Kelley was a fan and press favorite though it seemed too often that his "close but no cigar" finishes frustrated the difficult and often temperamental Boston media. After one of Kelly's second place finishes, the press ripped the Connecticut school teacher. Colin Heard of the *Boston Herald* wrote, "How stupid can a schoolteacher get?" John Gihooley of the *Boston Herald* also wrote, "If our schoolteachers are like that, it's no wonder our school system is in trouble."

His namesake, John "Elder" Kelley, finished in the top ten eighteen times including seven second places and two championships.

1991. As Peter Zimmerman, the lead American runner, worked his way into Boston, his sneaker began to fill with blood from broken blisters. From Coolidge Corner through Kenmore Square, he prayed for another American to pass him so that he could drop out of the race. Zimmerman was never passed by one of his countrymen, so he felt obligated to continue on to the finish line where he completed the race with his bloody sneakers in fourteenth place with a time of 2:15:32

The runners move past the intersection of Charlesgate West, under an overpass and then past Charlesgate East where the Leif Ericson statue greets them and inspires them to finish their journey. He faces away from the finish line, similar to the positioning of the Dough Boy statue back at the starting line.

After surviving Kenmore Square, the runners are greeted by the hysterical crowd of the Back Bay. Some are lining the streets while others are hanging out of apartment windows, and partying on the roofs of condominiums. The athlete who looked like a kid at Christmas back at the starting line, now looks more like a deserter from the French Foreign Legion here in the last mile.

The screams of "one more mile" are finally accurate.

Past the statue of Leif Ericson the runners stay right at the fork, and move past a small public park on their left. On the right stands the old Somerset Hotel and the Harvard Club. Here the members of the club used to cheer from a temporary grandstand set up in front of the club. Now they watch the race from inside on a big screen television, with the bar and grill open for the day. Next door to the Harvard Club is the Eliot Hotel, the old home of the famous Eliot Lounge.

The Eliot Lounge became famous in 1975 when winner Bill Rodgers told a national audience while being interviewed after winning the Marathon, "I'm going to the Eliot Lounge." I'm sure Tom Leonard made Rodgers his favorite drink—Blue Whale. At the end of 1996 the Eliot Lounge was sadly closed.

Crossing in front of the Eliot Hotel, the runners move over Massachusetts Avenue on their way towards the big right turn off Commonwealth Avenue.

From years 1897 to 1964, the competitors used to continue down Commonwealth Avenue and take a sharp

With Kenmore Square in the foreground and Boston's skyline in the background, runners are relieved to hear the crowd yell "One more mile!" Photo courtesy of the Boston Athletic Association.

right four blocks from Massachusetts Avenue onto Exeter Street.

From the turn onto Exeter, the runners proceeded straight up the street, passing over Newbury Street, then through Boylston Street to the finish line, which was situated outside of the Boston Athletic Association Clubhouse. (During the first two years, the race continued past the clubhouse and over Huntington Avenue to the Irvington Oval.)

In 1965, the finish of the race was moved to the shadow of the brand new fifty-floor Prudential Center. On Easter Sunday, the Prudential welcomed the public to an open house and on Monday they welcomed the runners of the Boston Marathon. The Prudential, situated on Boylston Street, forced the BAA to adjust the route in Hopkinton and at the turn from Commonwealth Avenue. With this spot used for the finish, the starting point was moved to the Ashland side of the town green in Hopkinton, and finishes after taking a right turn onto Hereford Street and left onto Boylston Street just one block from Massachusetts Avenue and the Eliot Lounge. This turn, like any of the sharp corners on the route, can really test the legs of the runners. At the top of Hereford Street, past Newbury Street, is a nasty little incline.

Seven-time wheelchair champion, Jean Driscoll, talked about the last mile with special affection. She noted that a building on the corner of Hereford and Commonwealth had the name of Driscoll engraved on it. She joked, "It must be my destiny to win with my name so boldly displayed near the finish line."

She went on to describe the final yards as a goose-bumped-filled experience that causes all the stress of the journey to disappear. "It's a euphoric feeling whenever anyone achieves a goal whether it's winning, beating a time or just finishing the race."

1982. Will Cloney and two other marathon officials chose the Harvard Club for a meeting with Marshall Medoff who was a prospective corporate broker for the race. Medoff claimed he was a close personal friend of Prince Rainier of Monaco and that he could raise close to a $1,000,000 in corporate sponsorship for the race. These funds would be used to enhance a race which was quickly losing its luster and world class runners to other races around the world.

After dinner and drinks, Medoff and party had tentatively agreed that he would be allowed him to keep any monies over $400,000. Soon after, the details of this agreement were disputed and had to be settled in an elongated court battle. After much court play and backdoor agreements, lawyers got rich and Cloney's decades of hard work would become somewhat tarnished by his ambitious but naïve attempt to bring the race up to par.

1897. John McDermott, the winner of the first marathon, ran into a little more traffic than he expected at the intersection of Massachusetts Avenue and Commonwealth Avenue. With less than a mile to go, McDermott found himself running in front of both a funeral procession and two trolleys bringing both of them to a halt as he continued on to victory.

Roberta Gibb runs through Kenmore Square during her landmark finish in 1966.
Photo courtesy of the Boston Athletic Association.

Bill Rodgers runs up Hereford Street towards Boylston Street and the 1975 championship.
Photo courtesy of FayFoto.

The crowd bends in an appropriate question mark formation in order to allow the runners to turn from Hereford Street onto Boylston Street. Photo courtesy of FayFoto.

1925. At the turn onto Exeter Street, leader Chuck Mellor spit out his wad of tobacco, which he had been chewing throughout the route, so he wouldn't have a protruding cheek as he was pictured crossing the finish line.

1935. As the runners turned on to Exeter Street, 75-year-old Edward Redman, a spectator, was so overwhelmed by the event, that he collapsed with a heart attack, badly cutting his chin in the process. The Wellesley native was taken to a nearby hospital where he was nursed back to health.

1939. Running up Exeter Street with the lead, the eccentric and sometimes hard-to-explain Tarzan Brown stopped short, took in the scene, looked around at the crowd, and moved on to the finish line.

1897. Before John McDermott entered the Irvington Oval, the crowd was treated to a number of track and field events in the BAA annual track and field handicap event. In the big event, the boys from Boston College upset the favorite Fordham College runners in the 100-yard dash. As McDermott entered the oval, he was said to finish with the speed and strength of a half-miler.

1987. In an effort to catch lead runner Toshihiko Seko, British runners Steve Jones and Geoff Smith teamed up in the last quarter of the race to close the gap. As they turned off Hereford Street and onto Boylston Street, Seko was approaching the finish line. So the team of Jones and Smith shook hands and wished each other well in their battle for second place which Jones eventually won by five seconds.

At the top of Hereford Street, the route turns left on to Boylston Street. Most runners have a difficult time negotiating the tight turn. Their spent legs force them to round off the corner on the far right side of the street. At this point, an upgrade undetectable to the eye, but registered on the legs, takes you to the Twenty-Six mile mark—and 385 yards from the finish line.

MPC: The thrill of taking the turn on to Boylston Street from Hereford Street, was mind-boggling. I knew at that point that I would conquer the route that had destroyed so many. The finish line was in sight. My goal and dream would soon be realized.

In his effort to be recognized by the BAA in 1977, Bob Hall races toward the finish line while being urged on by his sister. Photo courtesy of the Boston Athletic Association.

385 YARDS

385 yards—1155 feet—13860 inches—that's all that's left. Once on Boylston Street, the athletes pass the Prudential Building and its fountain where the runners who finished the race cool themselves on hot days, then the Lord and Taylor department store and the Lenox Hotel on the same side at the Boylston and Exeter intersection.

The Lenox Hotel has long been associated with the Boston Marathon because of its proximity to the finish line. When the race finished outside of the BAA clubhouse, the hotel's side door to Exeter Street was prominently displayed in a number of newspaper pictures of the race as the winner broke the tape. The hotel has 214 rooms and throws a barbecue party on the roof for their top clients on race day.

In 1986 the start and finish of the race were rearranged to accommodate the new sponsor of the race, John Hancock Financial Services. The starting line was moved back to Route 135 on the east side of Hopkinton's town green while the finish was moved down Boylston Street about a quarter of a mile to the Boston Public Library.

The Boston Public Library opened in 1854 and was the first publicly supported library in the world, the first library to lend out books, and the first to open branch sites throughout the city.

The library was designed by architect Charles Follen McKim, from New York, who used Paris structure, Henri Labrouste's Bibliotheque Ste. Genevieve as his model. He customized the library to fit in with the neighboring buildings—the Romanesque Trinity Church and the Italian Gothic Old South Church. In 1965, the library added the Johnson Building where the BAA clubhouse once stood in the first third of the century.

The library acts as a depository for Massachusetts and regional federal government documents, United States government patents and United Nations documents. It receives more than two million visitors a year and holds over six million books, three million government documents, ten million patents.

After overcoming a host of obstacles, Uta Pippig cherished the last steps of her third Boston Marathon Championship in 1996 by staring into the accompanying television camera and screaming in ecstasy. "Some people feel that I'm too emotional, but that's me. I feel a special connection with the people who line the streets to cheer and I want to show these people who are sharing in the moment that I appreciate them and the race."

After crossing Exeter Street, the race continues another hundred yards up to the finish line. The Old South Church steeple gives the runners a golf-like line from hundreds of yards away.

PART III

COOLING DOWN

Gerard Cote wins one of his four Boston Marathons as he crosses the finish line in 1944.
Photo courtesy of Boston Public Library Print Dept.

REJOICE! WE CONQUER.

Sara Mae Berman:"The wonderful thing about athletic achievement is that it is finite. There is no ambiguity. You did it, and no one can ever take that away from you."

"The race was a big success. There is assurance that this event will be an annual fixture." So announced a BAA official after the 1897 running of the American Marathon of the Boston Athletic Association.

And it has been an annual fixture. For a century, runners have worked their way through Hopkinton, Ashland, Framingham, Natick, Wellesley, Newton, Boston, Brookline and back into Boston in order to fulfill a dream held by runners throughout the world—to run Boston!

John "Younger" Kelley, 1957 winner:"I had to prove something to myself, I never figured out what the hell it was, but I did it."

For those who have crossed the finish line, the accomplishment is both physically exhilarating and psychologically uplifting. A destiny has been found and a goal has been met. Although most runners go unheralded, their willingness to accept the challenge and conquer it is enough of a laurel wreath. For a hundred years, the competitors of the Boston Marathon have exemplified physical and mental strength. Their many accounts of courage and feats of greatness continue to add to the allure of the world's greatest race. For a hundred years, runners have come to Boston to run Boston. Their determination and bravado help to inspire others to reach for greatness.

One memorable example: Vietnam veteran Eugene Roberts, in 1970, became the first wheelchair athlete ever to run the Boston Marathon. In just over seven hours, the Baltimore native finished the race by getting down out of his chair and using his two hands to pull himself across the line. While waiting for the race, Roberts and his twin brother tried to figure out if it would be more efficient to run by hand jockeying (using his two hands as crutches, and pulling his body forward), a method which he had previously completed only three miles in training, or by wheelchair, in which he had only completed one mile in his training. Roberts decided on the wheelchair and inspired thousands of people along the route. While passing Boston College, admiring students joined this courageous athlete in his march towards Boston. With night falling, Roberts and his entourage covered the last mile singing "Praise the Lord."

Eugene Roberts and his brother Jim are all smiles after Eugene became the first wheelchair competitor to conquer the Boston Marathon. Photo courtesy of Boston Public Library Print Dept.

1906. Tim Ford won the Boston Marathon at age 18, the youngest runner ever to win the race.

1930. Nineteen years after his first victory, Clarence DeMar won the race at age forty-one, the oldest competitor ever to break the tape.

1942. Local favorite Fred McGlone, the "Galloping Golfer," moved down Exeter Street in sixth place and fell to the ground for the third time. Frantically, he waved people away who were trying to aid him. Finally, a policeman who could stand it no longer, picked up McGlone and carried him across the finish line.

1971. Eight-year-old Tom Bassler of Palace Verdes, California, ran 26 miles and finished the race alongside his father.

1972. Sylvia Weiner ran the Marathon in a time of 3:47. Throughout the struggle, she called upon her survival instincts to meet the 26-mile challenge. Weiner had spent her youth trapped in the terror of a Nazi concentration camp. "I always wanted to live. I always had the will for it. Now I have victory."

1974. Dr. Hing Hua Chun of Honolulu, his wife Connie and their six children—Jerry, Hinky, Daven, May Lee, June and Joy, ranging from age nine to fifteen—all ran and completed the 26-mile journey to Boston.

1975. Bob Hall became the first wheelchair competitor to be recognized by the BAA. Will Cloney, the race director, promised Hall if he finished the race within three hours, he would be presented with a finisher's certificate. Hall's time was 2:58.

To participate in an event such as a marathon, one must have vision. This allows the athlete to reach beyond their normal abilities. This reach for the brass ring is a challenge that is difficult enough when it is simply personal. But for those runners who carry the burden and hopes of an entire nation on their backs, the pressures to succeed are monumental. Most return home unsuccessful. But for those who return with a Boston Marathon laurel wreath, their athletic status is upgraded to national hero.

In 1926, Johnny Miles returned with his parents to their home in Sydney Mines, Nova Scotia after winning his first of two Boston Marathon championships. As he stepped off the train, he was taken from the station to the local hotel on the shoulders of the townspeople. Later he appeared on the balcony of his hotel room to greet the people.

At the starting line in 1946, Stylianos Kyriakides, a citizen of Greece who years earlier had barely avoided being executed by the occupying Nazis, carried a hand written note in each hand. He read the first note before the starter's gun was shot: "Do or Die." Upon winning the race, he opened up his other fist and read the second note: "We Are Victorious!"

In the early decades of the race, Canadian and American runners controlled the breaking of the tape. In the forties, fifties and into the sixties, Japanese (eight), South Korean (two) and Finnish (seven) runners captured the laurel wreath. In the late eighties and through the nineties, no region has dominated the outcome of the Boston Marathon more than the runners from Africa. Over the last nine years, African runners have won eight championships including three by Cosmos Ndeti and three by Ibrahim Hussein. In 1996 the first eight fin-

Above: Champion John "Elder" Kelley crosses the finish line in 1935. Note that officials never put the tape up and that Kelley dropped his aunt's handkerchief just yards before crossing the line. Photo courtesy of Boston Public Library Print Dept. *Below:* In an effort that exemplifies the battle of the Boston Marathon, a 1992 competitor refuses to be denied. Photo courtesy of the *Boston Herald*/Jim Mahoney.

Uta Pippig breaks the tape with her third Boston Marathon championship in 1996. Photo courtesy of FayFoto.

ishers were from Africa; seven of the eight were from Kenya.

The Boston Marathon community was treated to a glimpse of the greatness which lay ahead for the African runners in 1963 when Ethiopians Abebe Bikila and Mamo Wolde came to Boston and almost grabbed the laurel wreath themselves before falling off their record pace at mile 20.

Although Bikila and Wolde weren't able to repeat their Olympic successes in Boston, a later generation of Africans has picked up the baton and raised it high.

Tommy Leonard offered his theory on why the African runners were controlling the outcomes of the recent races. "They're hungrier. They train harder. They are like the Taiwanese Little League team in baseball."

Dr. Martin from Georgia State theorized, "The African runners live together, eat together and train together. Each is pushed to become their country's national hero."

While athletes from other countries split their attention between a number of sports, with a concentration on higher profile sports athletes from less well-developed countries passionately gravitate towards inexpensive sports, such as soccer and long distance running.

Runs of courage and national pride are certainly dramatic events that help to make Boston a legend, but nothing produces goose bumps like the sight of two runners running side by side with just yards to go to the finish line.

Twenty-six miles, three hundred and eighty-five yards. Hopkinton seemed as though it was weeks ago. The runners lived each yard one at a time. As each step was completed, it quickly became a distant memory while each yard in front seemed to stretch farther away. The cold, the heat, the rain, the snow, the traffic, the spilled beers, the car fumes—all for this euphoric feeling of cross-

1989. George Meyers satisfied his goal of running and finishing the Boston Marathon. The only problem was that his welcoming party wasn't present to cheer him on. His wife, Doreen was nowhere to be found. While George walked aimlessly in search of his wife, a BAA official approached him, and asked if he was George Meyers. He responded, "Yes." The BAA official told George that his wife was in labor at a local hospital. George will always remember Patriot's Day 1989 as one of great satisfaction. He reached his goal of running the Boston Marathon and became the father of a three-pound-two ounce baby.

1996. In the ultimate commitment to the Boston Marathon and a dream, Swedish runner Humphrey Siesage died of a massive heart attack while crossing the finish line. His medal was sent to his family in Stockholm. Their sadness must be somewhat lessened by the fact that their loved one died achieving what few humans ever accomplish.

1906. Tim Ford beat David Kneeland by six seconds.

1971. Alvaro Mejia beat Pat McMahon by five seconds (Jock Semple swears that Mejia elbowed McMahon into the crowd at the corner of Hereford and Commonwealth).

1978. Bill Rodgers beat Jeff Wells by five seconds.

1982. Alberto Salazar beat Dick Beardsley by two seconds.

1988. Ibrahim Hussein beat Juma Ikangaa by one second.

ing a simple line. The runs in the morning, at lunch, at night in the dark, past the chasing dogs, the puddle-splashing cars, the cars that pulled out on to the crosswalk, the cars that played 'chicken with you'—all for this euphoric feeling of crossing a simple line.

But it's not a simple line. It's a mental and physical barrier that, when conquered, offers a feeling of exaltation which is incomparable.

MPC: During training runs and physical therapy sessions, I used to envision myself running down Boylston Street in an effort to convince myself that this all would be worth it. I wondered and dreamed how special the moment would be. The commitment and agony would be worth every step, every bead of sweat, every twinge of pain.

As I worked my way down Boylston Street, I was bewildered to find that the finish line was still so far away. I decided to keep my head down and just work each step. My brother, who fought hard to slow his pace to stay with me, started to get excited. "Pick them up and put 'em back down. You're doing it! You're gonna do it! Listen to the crowd they're all yelling for you. Keep it going!"

With about hundred yards to go and tears swelling in my eyes, a burst of wind hit me in the face which almost knocked me over. As I continued towards the finish line, I realized that I was living the dream that I had dreamed so often. I was running the last hundred yards of the Boston Marathon. It was one of those rare moments in life when dreams and reality become one.

As I crossed the finish line, I pumped my fist in the air twice with the last bit of strength I had left, and then leaned on my brother. Kevin simply responded, "You did it."

Will Cloney, director of the BAA, is determined not to let a college prankster cross the 1959 finish line.
Photo courtesy of Boston Public Library Print Dept.

TRIALS AND TRIBULATIONS

Over the years, the race has had many exciting occurrences and fabulous finishes. But in any hundred-year event, there are bound to be infamous moments that stick to the history of the race like glue. Whether by elements under the BAA's jurisdiction or uncontrollable outside forces, the Boston Marathon has been shaped by both the good and the bad.

From Hopkinton to Boston, the responsibility of maintaining order is a challenging task. Cars, dogs, trains, 1.5 million spectators and the police have played a chaotic role in the race and its outcome.

In probably the greatest Boston Marathon of all time, Alberto Salazar and Dick Beardsley battled each other and the sideline distractions in 1982.

Shortly after the halfway mark in Wellesley, an intoxicated fan took a swing at the runners. His fist barely missed Beardsley, but struck Salazar in the stomach, temporarily knocking the breath out of him. Salazar regained his breath, and the runners continued stride for stride into Kenmore Square. In the Square, another drunken fan grabbed at Beardsley's shirt, impeding his stride. Beardsley shook the fan off just in time to be sideswiped by the press bus. Beardsley was so infuriated, he pounded on the side of the bus in frustration.

Continuing down Commonwealth Avenue with barely a mile to go, Beardsley stepped in a pothole with depths that seemed to bring his foot close to the Chinese border. The obstacle turned out to be a blessing in disguise because it shook out a cramp that Beardsley had been hobbled with for some miles. Escaping from the pothole, he moved onto Hereford Street in chase of the leader Salazar. Between the two runners rode some ten motorcycle policeman. From here to the finish, Beardsley was impeded twice by the motorcycles, and was actually hit by one, forcing him to push away the bike and its officer.

Salazar went on to win the race by two seconds.

Although there have been instances when runners have been adversely affected by forces outside of the race, the runners themselves have been responsible for disreputable actions.

One winner, who wasn't a winner in 1980, was Rosie Ruiz. Ruiz, born Maria Rosales in Havana, Cuba before settling in New York City, chose "marathoning" as a vehicle to bring attention upon herself. After obtaining New York Marathon credentials through fraudulent means, she convinces her boss to pay her way to Boston to run the

famous Boston Marathon. So with her fraudulent cer-
tification from New York, she applied and obtained an
official number from the BAA.

She started the race with the other competitors in
Hopkinton. Somewhere on the course she peeled away
from the route, only to re-enter just past Kenmore Square
where she raced towards the finish line. She crossed
with a time of 2:31 which qualified for the third fastest
time ever run by a woman.

Throughout the course, Canadian runner
Jacqueline Gareau was told by people that she was run-
ning in first. Even television commentator Kathy
Switzer, who had followed the women's field by vehicle,
yelled to Gareau, close to the twenty-two mile mark,
"You're in the lead." When Gareau turned on to Boylston
Street just yards from her greatest moment, she was
shocked to hear the public address speaker refer to her
as the second place female runner.

But how could this be? No one had ever heard of
Rosie Ruiz. Bill Rodgers asked her on the podium, "How
are you? Who are you?" Rodgers later said, "Think of
the most famous marathon runners—Pheideppides and
Rosie Ruiz—one dropped dead and the other was crazy."

Ruiz had not been spotted at any of the check-
points. Her shirt was almost dry and her knowledge of
running was elementary. At the press conference when
Kathy Switzer, an analyst for a local television station
that year, grilled her on topics such as intervals and
training, Ruiz was vague and unresponsive. She was
eventually stripped of the championship, but she refused
to return the winner's medal. Gareau was cheated of
her championship glory.

A week later she flew in from Canada, and ran
the final two hundred yards in a pair of jeans. Two
hundred people cheered her on while Bill Rodgers held
her arm up in victory.

THE OBSTACLE COURSE

1901. Runners lost minutes off their time when they were forced to detour around the crowds of thirty deep, on Exeter Street.

1905. Winner Fred Lorz had to leap a bike (for the second time) at the finish line. While leaping, he caught his foot and crashed through the finish line tape onto Exeter Street.

1907. In their hurry to control the crowd, police almost ran over the leader, Tom Longboat.

1929. After winning the race, Johnny Miles wrote the following day in the *Boston Globe*, "It was not only a battle against a great runner, but a battle against fumes of gasoline, automobiles, motorcycles which were often to close for comfort and a dog who jumped at me before Coolidge Corner, and scared me."

1941. The loud crowd spooked a pony, causing him to chase the leader, Les Pawson, up Exeter Street towards the finish line until it was caught and brought under control.

1962. After a dog knocked down John "Younger" Kelley the prior year, the pre-race talk focused on the control of dogs along the route. A similar discussion was held in 1910 with regard to controlling trains after trains crossed the route and cut off runners in South Framingham during the 1907 and 1909 races. In 1956, pre-race talk again centered on subjects other than the runners which played factors in the outcome. This year the use of cars was a major issue.

1978. In his 47th race at the age 70, John "Elder" Kelley complained that the crowd in Framingham and Natick were squeezing the runners into single file causing a back up. "If we weren't bunched up, I could have broken 3:30. I love this race and the people but the runners need to be able to run."

In the same race, during the great duel between Bill Rodgers and Jeff Wells (which Rodgers won by five seconds), the official bus and press bus finished sixth and seventh in the race behind the top five runners. Throughout the race, the bus trailed the leaders thereby denying the leaders the opportunity to calculate and monitor splits throughout the classic duel.

IMAGINATIVE INITIATIVES

1909. Howard Pearce of New Bedford was rushing towards the tape amidst the cheers of thousands of spectators, when a police sergeant tackled him moments before he ran over the finish line. Pearce, the apparent leader, had jumped into a car in Wellesley and had hitched a ride to Kenmore Square where he re-entered the race. Many policemen, unaware that he had cheated, cheered him on and moved the crowd back. Luckily, an alert sergeant stepped in and prevented Pearce from experiencing the thrill that he didn't deserve.

1916. The fifth place finisher, A.F. Merchant, was seen by a race volunteer getting into a car on Beacon Street. Merchant denied the boy's accusations.

Later she visited the Eliot Lounge where Tommy Leonard was ready for her. With a bottle of Dom Perignon on ice, the Canadian flag flew solo over the bar. As she walked in, one of the bar patrons got on the piano and played "Oh Canada." Leonard later said, "There wasn't a dry eye in the house."

In a 1997 Marathon finish that was too good to be true, John (60) and Suzanne Murphy (59), a husband and wife team who had won their respective age categories, were disqualified when they failed to show up on video at any of the checkpoints throughout the course.

With a constant headwind throughout the race, John and Suzanne Murphy submitted finishing times in 1997 that were 11 and 12 minutes faster than their 1996 Boston Marathon times.

The rightful winners Anthony Cerminaro and Susan Gustafson were eventually recognized as the winners of the men's senior category and the women's veterans group.

Ultimately the BAA is responsible for the race and all that happens within it. The BAA continues to learn and grow from each experience, but when their shortcomings are exposed, the roar is loud and shrill.

Jerome Drayton, of Canada, who had just won the 1977 Boston Marathon, crossed the finish line, stopped and looked back at the race route with disgust. He briefly wore the laurel wreath before taking it off as if Drayton's association with this race would bring great shame upon his family. He moved from the finish line to the press conference, where he vented his frustration upon the course, the spectators and the BAA.

He complained that the start was disorganized and that people grabbed his shirt and kicked him in the calf. Throughout the route, there were sporadic and unmarked water stops, he claimed, and mileage signs were small and inconspicuous.

Checkpoints were at odd spots and made it hard for the runners to calculate splits. He scoffed, mocked and ridiculed a race which was more than a race, to the people of Boston and Massachusetts. How dare he come into our home, run our race, take our championship and turn his nose up at us. He had a nerve.

This show of arrogance turned out to be somewhat called for and justified. It turned out to be a sorely-needed wake-up call for the BAA.

Current race director Guy Morse: "The situations involving Jerome Drayton and Rosie Ruiz caught our attention."

Tom Leonard, the guru of the Boston Marathon, echoed the call of the runners:"The Boston Marathon is a vintage wine which should have a delicate bouquet. The race has a million dollar audience and a twenty-five cent field."

The brother of four-time winner Bill Rodgers, Charlie, expressed his distaste for the race's organizers:"The race itself is exciting. If you want to talk about the BAA— well, they're losers."

In the early days, this race was the only race around. Criticisms were ignored or disregarded. Other than the Olympics, the runners had no place to go to showcase their skills.

As the marathon craze grew exponentially in the seventies, the effort to conduct the Marathon in a safe and responsible fashion became a growing concern. A laurel wreath, some gauze on the bottom of some feet

1927. Several runners, who had earlier dropped out of the race, jumped back on the course, after being transported by an undetermined vehicle, between the second and third place runners. Their actions spoiled the experience of finishing third for past winner, William Kennedy.

1950. Police sargent Ed Fallon failed in his attempt to stop Dick Stevens, an MIT fraternity boy, from crossing the finish line. Stevens, who had jumped into the race just in front of the finish line, dove past the policeman, cutting his knees but experiencing the thrill of crossing the line.

❧❧❧❧❧

1927. In 1926, the BAA provided water stops for the runners. These relief spots were rarely utilized causing the BAA to cancel the water stops for 1927. In that year's race, temperatures climbed into the mid-80s. Dehydration was a major problem.

1941. Two Harvard runners, Douglas Shepardson and Edmund Souder, ran the Marathon on a bet with their Crimson classmates. At the end of the race, in which they brought up the rear, they voiced their displeasure that there weren't more official water stops. Over the 26-mile route, the two runners received no water and one orange.

Jacqueline Gareau has her hand lifted in victory by men's winner Bill Rodgers one week after the 1980 race. Gareau was a victim of the underhanded actions of Rosie Ruiz. Photo courtesy of FayFoto.

1935. John "Elder" Kelley arrived at the finish line before the officials had positioned the tape across the line, thus denying Kelley the thrill of breaking the tape in victory.

1946. After city workers completed painting the finish line, a hook and ladder fire engine, racing to a fire, crossed over the line leaving white tire tracks down the right and left side of the finish.

1972. Because of "skimpy personnel," Newton-Wellesley Hospital was called to assist in picking up stranded runners who were in need of help on the side of the route.

and a shake of the hand wasn't going to do it anymore. Racers were waiting for the BAA to grow the race into a first class international event. That meant bringing professionalism to the greatest amateur event, next to the Olympics, in a town that doesn't take change very well. Boston was built on Swan Boats, Irish politicians, baked beans, the losing Red Sox and a number of men running a race in April for the thrill of competition. But, there was no doubt that the race was in dire need of a tune up.

The BAA and race director Will Cloney eventually heeded the cries for help. That's when he turned to Marshall Medoff. In 1981, the BAA crossed the line and sought financial support from corporate sponsors. Throughout Boston and the racing community, Medoff's "pimp-like" methods created much animosity. Eventually the responsibility as the middle man for the race's sponsorship was ripped from Medoff's hands and placed directly into the financially capable hands of John Hancock Financial Services Company.

In the years leading up to 1986, the first year of Hancock's involvement, the quality of the field was beginning to diminish. The world class runners were turning to many of the alternative marathons in an effort to promote themselves and their sneakers. They needed a reason to return to Boston.

John Hancock gave them that reason in the form of prize money and appearance money for attending running clinics on the Saturday and Sunday before the race. (Along with the prize money for winning the race, money may be awarded to runners for breaking time barriers, world records and course records.)

The world class runners did return to Boston, thus fostering its legacy for the next hundred years.

Rival marathon organizers in Chicago were upset with the renewed spirit in Boston (brought on by the relationship between Hancock and the Boston Marathon). They felt that appearance money caused the runners to "lose the fire in their belly."

Whether or not the criticism is legitimate, there is no question that the Boston Marathon had lost a piece of its innocence and purity with the injection of professionalism. The Boston Marathon was now in the real world, forced to compete in a dog-eat-dog market that required it to sell a piece of its soul in order to stay alive.

With the funding provided by John Hancock, the race has been revitalized with a new spirit and a high quality of competition and organization.

THE WINNERS' REWARDS

Once the line is crossed, the winner is crowned with the laurel wreath and presented with gifts (such as a punch bowl, bronze statue, gold medal studded with diamonds, goblets, automobiles and money).

The list below represents a break down of 1996 award money presented to the winners of each category.

	Men & women open division	Masters	Wheelchair
1st Place	$100,000	$12,000	$12,000
2nd Place	$ 50,000	$ 6,000	$ 6,000
3rd Place	$ 25,000	$ 3,000	$ 3,000

The setting of new world and course records can add up to $75,000 to the pot. The awards' grand total is valued at an unprecedented $600,000.

After the winner crosses the finish line, the post-race activities attempt to move according to plan, but sometimes it's better left to flow at its own speed. Race officials had to delay the 1907 ceremonies in order to get the winner to stop running. Tom Longboat, of Hamilton, Ontario finished the race outside the BAA in great shape. From there, he proceeded to enter the BAA gym and run laps around the indoor track. Finally, officials convinced Longboat to slow down to a walk in fear he might drop dead of a heart attack.

In 1954 English runner Jim Peters, who was the fastest marathoner in the world at that time, finished the race in second place. Upon crossing the line, Jock Semple picked up Peters on his hip, in an attempt to carry him into the clubhouse. Semple lost his balance, dropping Peters and almost cracking the runner's skull on the curbside. Nine years later, BAA officials attempted to whisk the winner, Aurele Vandendriessche of Belgium, away from the crowd in an effort to administer the post-race physical. Instead he pushed the officials away, discarded his draped blanket, and proceeded to mingle with the crowd like a presidential candidate disobeying his Secret Service agents.

Since 1987, the laurel wreath that is awarded to the winners has been cut from a Kotinos tree just outside of Marathon, Greece and then flown to Boston for the awards ceremony. This coveted symbol of victory has been the object of

Ellison "Tarzan" Brown proudly fashions his laurel wreath after winning the second of his two Boston Marathons in 1939. Photo courtesy of Boston Public Library Print Dept.

larceny, pride and indifference. In an effort to earn money during trying times, New Hampshire resident and 1909 Boston Marathon champion Henri Renaud lent his most coveted laurel wreath and trophy to a carnival that had set up camp in his town. After several days on exhibit, Renaud was distraught to wake up one morning and find the carnival, wreath and trophy had all left town in the middle of the night.

Three decades later as "Tarzan" Brown showered in the Boston University Gym after his 1939 win, a heartless sports fan snuck into his bag and stole his winner's wreath.

In 1945 fellow runners and media members tried to convince winner John "Elder" Kelley to send his laurel wreath to Eleanor Roosevelt as a sign of sympathy for the passing of her husband, President Franklin Roosevelt. Kelley retorted, "I think the wreath has more significance to me than it would for Mrs. Roosevelt."

After winning his fifth championship in 1995, Jim Knaub sought out a young child in order to give the youth his laurel wreath as a memento of the race. Knaub, who doesn't keep any of his trophies, explained, "Admiring my trophies or daydreaming of past accomplishments is an act of looking backwards. For me, I have to continue to move forward. I'm afraid if I look back I might stop moving forward. It's like running a race—just concern yourself with what's ahead—anything behind you doesn't matter."

Over the years, representatives of Greece have frequently been chosen to crown the winner, strengthening the link between the 1896 Olympic Games in Athens and the Boston Marathon.

In conjunction with the individual awards, the BAA presents team awards to the athletic club with the lowest score. Points are assigned according to the runners' finish in the race: first place one point, second place two points; etc. Over the years, distinguished clubs added substantially to the history of the marathon, including Boston Athletic Association, Mohawk Athletic Club (NY), Cambridgeport Athletic Club, Meadowbrook Athletic Club (PA), Dorchester Running Club, Millrose Athletic Club, North Medford Athletic Club, German-American Athletic Club, United States Machinery Athletic Club, Toronto Monarches, Boston Edison Employee Club, Gladstone Athletic Club (Canada) Toronto, San Blas Club (Puerto Rico), Washington Track Club. In 1996, the Central Park Club "Team A" won the Male Open Team Championship while the Forerunners T.C. from Florida won the Female Open Team Championship.

After the gifts are awarded, the press needs to be satisfied. There have been times when the pressure of meeting deadlines produced indecorous behavior. In 1976, after running through one of the hottest races in the history of the event, overheated champion Jack Fultz was hurried into the press conference without an opportunity to cool down or stretch out. There he was thrown into a barber's chair and peppered with questions for over an hour. When he finally got up, he could barely keep his feet.

But usually the press conference is a monotonous affair, although the repetition provides a common thread from year to year. Each year the press asks the same questions and the runners reply with the same answers. Only the faces change: "How do you feel? When did you know you had it won? Are you happy?"—"I feel great. I could run another marathon! I knew I had it won when I crossed the finish line. Yes, I'm happy." Here are some of the more memorable summations:

After winning his fourth championship in 1948, Gerard Cote of Quebec told the press, "Gentlemen, Gentlemen! One beer! One cigar! Then we can talk about the race!"

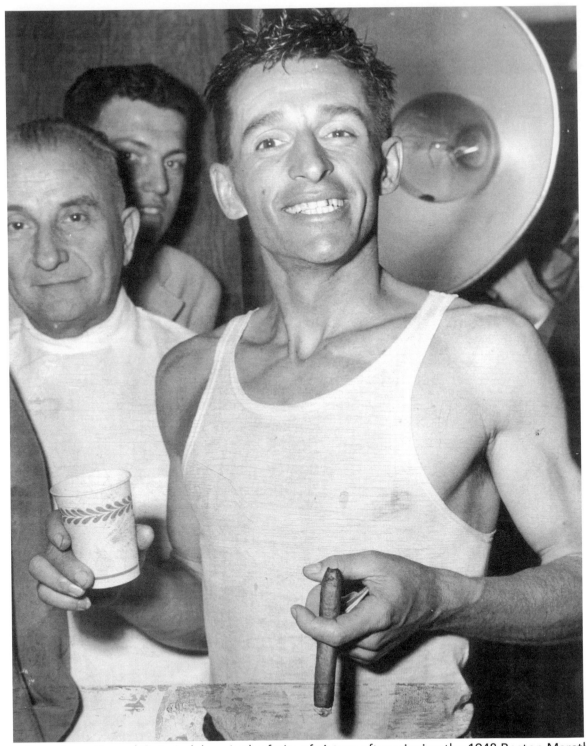

Four-time winner Gerard Cote indulges in the fruits of victory after winning the 1948 Boston Marathon.
Photo courtesy of Boston Public Library Print Dept.

In 1968, Amby Burfoot recounted his run as the perfect run. "From the moment the gun sounded, I ran with an ease that I had never experienced. I felt like I was running beyond my means while at the same time staying within myself. I can only explain my run as one of supreme effortlessness."

1976 winner Jack Fultz: "My run was so relaxed and comfortable that I was concerned that I wasn't pushing myself enough. But when I finally came upon a clock I was on the exact pace that I had hoped."

In 1978 Gayle Barron looked back on her run. "I had run a number of marathons previous to '78. In each of those races, I always would be afflicted with some type of ailment, whether it be blisters, cramps or something worse. This year everything worked perfectly. I ran like I had never run before. Each mile was quicker than I had ever run but I felt like I was in a light jog. I remember being on the winner's podium and being shocked. I could have kept going. I felt perfect. The day was perfect."

Cosmas Ndeti: "This isn't just another race. Boston is special. There is something magic about the race."

The Boston Marathon beats up yet another challenger. Photo courtesy of the Boston Athletic Association.

THE PHYSICAL AFTERMATH

Dr. Marvin Adner, Medical Director for the Marathon: "The last thing you should do to be healthy is run a marathon."

After the race is over, the runners have to tend to their overstrained bodies. Until the 1960s, each competitor was examined by a physician before the start of the race. During the event, the doctors would be chauffeured, by train or motor car, to the finish where they would again poke and prod the athletes in order to declare each in good health. Each exam would include: a listen of the heart and the lungs; a jump on the scale to figure out how much weight the runner had lost during the race; and, in some years a heart X-ray so that the doctors could judge whether marathon running had a negative impact on the human body. Usually, the doctor would smile and declare to the press, "All are healthy other than some loss of weight and blisters on the feet."

A quick listen with a stethoscope, and jump on a scale was acceptable when there were five hundred runners. Since those days, post-race medical facilities have matured into a full-scale triage area which more closely resembles a MASH unit after a violent battle, instead of a place for runners. Filled with cots, medical nurses, IV nurses, intravenous therapists, podiatrists, cardiologists, intensive care personnel, and drug testing officials, a runner is in good hands if not good feet.

MPC: After crossing the finish line, I had an overwhelming desire to fall asleep. Medical personnel recommended that I take a detour into the medical tent and regain my faculties. With a drained body, stiff knee, blisters on my feet and chills, I concurred with their diagnosis.

When my brother left to find me some dry clothes, a nurse attended to me. After I was placed near a heater and covered with three blankets, my system started to return to normal. Before I was allowed to go, I was required to drink 24 ounces of Gatorade, 12 ounces of water and 12 ounces of cold chicken soup. After consuming enough fluids to tip me over, two physical therapists made me take a swing around the tent to assure them that I was capable of walking. With the lap completed and the fluids finished, I was allowed to venture outside to find my family at the Boston Common a mile down Boylston Street. As I walked down the street, with two Mylar blankets taped around me like capes, a well-meaning girl offered me a Power Bar. I felt like saying, "I don't need a Power Bar. I need to be read my last rites!

It was almost six o'clock and the sun was down. The temperature had plummeted into the low 40s and the wind was howling. The thought of doing another mile was out of the question. Luckily a volunteer saw me and offered me a ride to the Common in a wheelchair. There I found my wife, son, and brother—the loneliness of the marathon route was over.

Dr Lyle Micheli, captain of the finish line medical team.: "Marathon running is a very special sport; it's something you don't play games with. You have to really respect that event."

After the rush of adrenaline subsides, the competitors start to realize that they have just overextended their bodies. Many a marathoner has sat on a bus or medical cot, or in a hotel room and has thought, "Never again will I do this to myself."

Frank Shorter: "You can't think of your next marathon until you've forgotten your last one."

After working the finish line for the *Boston Globe*, sportswriter Dan Shaughnessy invoked the inverted rule of finish theory in his column the following day: "The longer you wait, the worse shape the runners are in."

The number of competitors in need of medical care is usually a function of the weather more than any other factor. A hot day is not only the runners' nightmare but also that of the doctors, attendants and nurses who are responsible for providing care along the route.

Alberto Salazar pushed himself to the limit in his 1982 championship run for the wreath. Second place finisher, Dick Beardsley, kept whispering, "I took him to the finish." Salazar was whispering, "I don't feel so good."

Salazar ended up in the garage of the Prudential Center, which acted as the makeshift infirmary for the walking wounded of the marathon. Salazar, suffering from hypothermia, had his temperature drop to 88 degrees. Doctors and IV nurses injected three liters of 5%

1905. After the usual post-marathon physicals, Dr. Blake bemoaned that a number of the runners finished in a bad way. He continued, "they [the runners] can blame their handlers for this. These men were given whiskey on the journey, which is a bad thing. The men who didn't take alcoholic stimulants fared much better."

1986. Tony Chamberlain, a writer from the *Boston Globe*, witnessed the scene in the medical area after the race. He reported, "There were cries of pain, shoes full of blood, gaunt mummies walking around—it resembled a scene from a war."

1996. The following is a list of the medical supplies at the finish line for the 100th running: 15,000 Mylar blankets, 1,500 flannel blankets, 800 wool blankets, 10,000 plastic adhesive strips, 10,000 gauze pads, 3,000 bandages, 3,000 roll of tapes, 11,000 cold cups, 8,000 hot cups, 180 gallons of drinking water, 3,500 bags of intravenous fluids, 1,500 intravenous needles, 400 bottle of wound disinfectant, 16 defibrillators and 8 gallons of massage lotion.

❧ ❧ ❧ ❧ ❧

1897. John McDermott, the winner of the first race, told the press that this would be his last long distance race. He said "I hope you don't think I'm a coward or a quitter but look at my [blistered] feet." McDermott lost eight pounds over the course.

1976. Kim Merritt, winner of the Women's Open division, was reported to say after the race, "I don't know if I'd do it over again." She was later taken to the hospital for observation.

❧❧❧❧❧

1909. When the temperature hit 97 degrees, 91 runners in a field of 164, dropped out of the race.

1927. Runners throughout the route dropped out as thermometers registered more than 80 degrees. At the end, doctors reported several cases of heat stroke and three cases of heart dilation. Defending champion Johnny Miles was a "pitiful sight," reported the Boston Globe, on Miles' being carried to the finish in a motor car.

1985. Approximately 2000 runners were treated by medical personnel when the afternoon sun moved the mercury above 70 degrees.

1993. With the temperature approaching 80 degrees, medical personnel were forced to use almost 800 IV bags in an effort to revitalize spent runners.

dextrose/Saline IV's in each of Salazar's arms in an attempt to bring his temperature back to normal.

Physical punishment was not unusual for Salazar. During the Falmouth Road Race the previous August, Salazar was taken off the course, with a temperature of 108 degrees. He was quickly placed in a rubber raft with a hundred pounds of ice in an attempt to bring down his body temperature. Suffering from hyperthermia, Salazar slipped into a coma and was given the last rites. Salazar lived to run again, but after Boston he never was the same.

Ray Hosler.: "After 26 miles of running, you either feel like a conquered hero, or a defeated and bludgeoned victim."

Jessie Van Zant, Ollie Mannienen, Gerard Cote (winner), John Kelley, Ted Vogel are more than happy to rest their sore and blistered feet following the 1948 race. Photo courtesy of Boston Public Library Print Dept.

ICE BAGS, COLD BEER AND STIFF MUSCLES

Uta Pippig, "After the race is over, I like to stop by a couple of parties and enjoy the other competitors. I really respect all of the runners. Like a woman who breaks 4:10 for the first time. She might have a full-time job and a family, but she met and defeated a challenge. That is a great accomplishment."

After the race is finished, the wreaths are presented and the injuries are tended to. In the early days bowls of beef stew were provided, except on Good Friday when the runners were treated to fish cakes and fish chowder. The runners are ready to celebrate. Modern-day activities start around six o'clock, thus giving the runner the opportunity to cool down and relax. Winners and celebrities stay busy answering to the press and well-wishers. For some, the time lapse poses a problem because of their need to check out of hotel rooms. Others have to keep going after the race, or their bodies will not regenerate the energy needed to get dressed and go out some three hours later.

Before the Eliot Lounge closed, Tommy Leonard used to give a free beer to any runners who showed their numbers. The winners and Team Hoyt usually stopped by for a beer and Ricky was usually given a victor's ride on the patron's shoulders to a comfortable seat for a well-deserved beer.

At six o'clock, the Copley Plaza holds the awards dinner in the Grand Ballroom. At the same time, Dave McGillivray, the technical director of the race, is starting his run from Hopkinton to Boston after tying up any loose ends. His run is a little more difficult because of his hectic day, and because cars have been allowed back on the route.

Following the awards ceremony at the Copley, there are parties at the local dance clubs and hotels for those who can still move their legs. For the 100th running, Landesdown Street, just outside of Kenmore Square, was turned into a mini-version of Bourbon Street in New Orleans.

Micky Lawrence, of Image Impact: "This type of post-party event gives the experience some closure. Psychologists have told us that an endeavor of this magnitude demands some type of forum for competitors to ease their emotions with other individuals who shared their experience."

Here is how some of the athletes "experienced closure" over the years:

1926 winner Clarence DeMar returned to his hometown of Melrose to find the bells in the town center in full chime. The town turned out to greet its hero and shake the hand of the man who put them on the map. When

DeMar was through with the greetings, he went home and had supper with his mother. He then changed and went out and played a baseball game two hours after finishing the race.

After winning his fifth championship in 1927, DeMar was brought to a Melrose movie theater in order to greet his Boy Scout troop. When DeMar walked in, the boys almost tore off the roof.

Eddie Mack, from the Boston Garden, invited and hosted the 1929 runners at boxing matches that were held the night of the race.

1935 winner John Kelley was driven to his parents home in Arlington compliments of the local police force, who had their sirens blaring. The fire station rang bells 39 times in recognition of Kelley's winning the 39th Boston Marathon.

In 1946, Harvard first baseman Bill Fitz finished the race in ragged shape. He proceeded to change his clothes and make his way over to Soldiers Field where Harvard was in extra innings against the University of Connecticut. His coach asked him if he could pinch hit. He said, "Yes, but if I get on, I need a pinch runner."

1959 winner Eino Oksanen from Finland was spotted doing the polka at 12:30 p.m. in a Quincy, Massachusetts social club nine hours after his first championship.

1979 winners Bill Rodgers and Joan Benoit were invited to the White House to have dinner with President Jimmy Carter. Depending on the President's interests, runners are now customarily invited to run with the President.

After winning, Uta Pippig has a great feeling of relief. "I feel good for myself and for the people who gave up so much to support me. In training, you have shut yourself off from so many people who are important in your life. Now I know I'll have the opportunity to reunite with them."

THE NEXT HUNDRED YEARS

Where does the race go from here? What country will turn out the next generation of world class marathoners? Will the African nations continue their mastery of the road from Hopkinton to Boston? Will John Hancock Financial Services keep coming back to the table? Will there ever be another Johnny Kelley? Will the people of Hopkinton who oppose the marathon gain momentum in their town? What will the next hundred years hold for the modern world's oldest race?

Change means new and uncharted waters. Change is scarey to New Englanders. We like to know where we're going and how we're going to get there. Electric scoreboards at Fenway Park, the renovation of the Boston Garden, and the demolition of the elevated train system didn't come about without a fight. But somehow we survive and even sometimes privately admit that change can be for the better. Women runners, wheelchair competitors, revised checkpoints, frequent water stops, prize money, the BAA unicorn on the face of commercial products, and adjustments to the route are all changes that have enhanced the Boston Marathon.

Guy Morse of the BAA:

The by-laws of the Boston Athletic Association, which was established in 1887, state that the "exclusive purposes of the Association shall be the promotion of the common good and health and welfare of the general public and the encouragement of the general public to improve their physical condition by the promotion and regulatin of amatuer sports competition, with particular emphasis on the sponsorship of long distance running events [especially the traditional annual Boston Athletic Assocation Marathon] and of the track and field teams and meets and similar athletic exercises."

As with most event that have withstood the test of time, the Boston Marathon's success has been the result of a combination of factors. We have been innovative in the race's technical support. The support of our communities, and dedication of runners, together with the durability of the Boston Athletic Association through changing times and sometimes criticism have brought about strong leadership and organization. Of course we have benefitted from certain intangibles such as a fair amount of good luck and fate, as well.

So as change swirls around us, we take comfort in the fact that the beauty of the Boston Marathon experience remains the same. Runners still venture west of Boston to compete in an endurance event that pushes the limits of the mind and body. At the same time, generations of New Englanders and running fans from all over the world continue to line the roads traveled by their forerunners a century ago.

A simple medal that means the world. Photo courtesy of FayFoto.

EPILOGUE

Amby Burfoot:"Boston was everything in my eyes. Boston was, to me, more important than the Olympics. Boston was in my blood. It had to be Boston."

MPC:After finding my family, I hailed a cab that carried us straight home. My wife made a delicious dinner that I had difficulty keeping down. Later, I sank into a nice hot tub where I discovered that I had a bad sunburn on the back of my legs.

Around eight o'clock, Richie called to see how I had done. We were both excited to hear that all four of us had been successful in reaching the finish line. If one of us had dropped out of the race, it would have tarnished the experience knowing that we all had worked so hard yet hadn't all shared the exhilaration of finishing. Richie then recalled an event six months earlier when we had put our hands together like the three musketeers and vowed to each other to run the Boston Marathon. We were true to our vow.

Five minutes later Michael and Jack Radley came by to make sure I still had a pulse. They were sore and tired but smiling. I was glad they had come by—I needed some closure to the event. I was glad to see and hear from my three comrades. So again we shook hands and parted with a special bond that would last a lifetime.

Fifteen minutes later I settled into bed with a sunburn on my legs, an injured knee and a tired body. At that time, I allowed myself to revel in the beginning of perpetual self-glorification. I replayed the race over and over again in my head, and got goose bumps every time I crossed the finish line. Even months later, when I pass over the marathon course, I find myself saying "I did it."

All my whining and complaining comes with the territory, but every step was worth it. Fulfillment comes in many shapes and colors. The ability to run the Boston Marathon creates a profound and unique feeling of physical and mental fulfillment.

For 364 days of the year, the route from Hopkinton to Boston is simply a 26-mile stretch of pavement and sidewalk, not much different than other 26-mile roads. But on the day of the Boston Marathon, the road from Hopkinton to Boston comes alive with a pounding pulse and passionate heart. Referred to by some as alluring and seductive and by others as heartbreaking, this course has a romantic enchantment for both the competitors and the spectators.

For more than 100 years, the images of the Boston Marathon have been ingrained into the souls of those who came to challenge, conquer or cheer. The visions and memories endure—Clarence DeMar's proud chest breaking the tape, Uta Pippig's radiant Boylston Street smile, Bill Rodgers gloved hands, Johnny Kelley's immortal stride, and the sight of a small boy on his father's shoulders—offer unforgettable images of the Boston Marathon.

For the competitor, the race has significance beyond a road race. It is a love affair. It is a link to our past. It is tradition and innocence. It is the one day of the year where representatives from every corner of the world share a bond. From every walk of life, individuals come to run, to watch and to follow a dream on the 365th day.

MEN'S OPEN CHAMPIONS

YEAR	NAME/RESIDENCE	TIME			
1897	John J. McDermott, New York City	2:55:10	1930	Clarence DeMar, Melrose, MA	2:34:48
1898	Ronald J. MacDonald, Cambridge, MA	2:42:00	1931	James Hennigan, Medford, MA	2:46:45
1899	Lawrence J. Brignolia, Cambridge, MA	2:54:38	1932	Paul de Bruyn, Germany	2:33:36
1900	John Caffery, Hamilton, Ontario	2:39:44	1933	Leslie S. Pawson, Pawtucket, RI	2:31:01
1901	John Caffery, Hamilton, Ontario	2:29:23	1934	Dave Komonen, Sudbury, Ontario	2:32:53
1902	Sammy Mellor, Yonkers, NY	2:43:12	1935	John A. Kelley, Arlington, MA	2:32:07
1903	John C. Lorden, Cambridge, MA	2:41:29	1936	Ellison (Tarzan) Brown, Alton, RI	2:33:40
1904	Michael Spring, New York City	2:38:04	1937	Walter Young, Verdun, Quebec	2:33:20
1905	Fred Lorz, New York City	2:38:25	1938	Leslie S. Pawson, Pawtucket, RI	2:35:34
1906	Timothy Ford, Cambridge, MA	2:45:45	1939	Ellison (Tarzan) Brown, Alton, RI	2:28:51
1907	Tom Longboat, Hamilton, Ontario	2:24:24	1940	Gerard Cote, St. Hyacinthe, Quebec	2:28:28
1908	Thomas Morrissey, New York City	2:25:43	1941	Leslie S. Pawson, Pawtucket, RI	2:30:38
1909	Henri Renaud, Nashua, NH	2:53:36	1942	Bernard Joseph Smith, Medford, MA	2:26:51
1910	Fred Cameron, Amherst, Novia Scotia	2:28:52	1943	Gerard Cote, St. Hyacinthe, Quebec	2:28:25
1911	Clarence H. DeMar, Melrose, MA	2:21:39	1944	Gerard Cote, St. Hyacinthe, Quebec	2:31:50
1912	Mike Ryan, New York City,	2:21:18	1945	John A. Kelley, Arlington, MA	2:30:40
1913	Fritz Carlson, Minneapolis, MN	2:25:14	1946	Stylianos Kyriakides, Greece	2:29:27
1914	James Duffy, Hamilton, Ontario	2:25:01	1947	Yun Bok Suh, South Korea	2:25:39
1915	Edouard Fabre, Montreal, Quebec	2:31:41	1948	Gerard Cote, St. Hyacinthe, Quebec	2:31:02
1916	Arthur Roth, Roxbury, MA	2:27:16	1949	Karl Gosta Leandersson, Sweeden	2:31:50
1917	William Kennedy, Port Chester, NY	2:28:37	1950	Ki Yong Ham, South Korea	2:32:39
1918	Camp Devens Divisional Team	2:24:53	1951	Shigeki Tanaka, Japan	2:27:45
1919	Carl Lidner, Quincy, MA	2:29:13	1952	Doroteo Flores, Guatemala	2:31:53
1920	Peter Trivoulidas, Greece	2:29:31	1953	Keizo Yamada, Japan	2:18:51
1921	Frank Zuna, Newark, NJ	2:18:57	1954	Veikko Karvonen, Finland	2:20:39
1922	Clarence DeMar, Melrose, MA	2:18:10	1955	Hideo Hamamura, Japan	2:18:22
1923	Clarence DeMar, Melrose, MA	2:23:37	1956	Antti Viskari, Finland	2:14:14
1924	Clarence DeMar, Melrose, MA	2:29:40	1957	John J. Kelley, Groton, CT	2:20:05
1925	Charles Mellor, Chicago, IL	2:33:00	1958	Franjo Mihalic, Yugoslavia	2:25:54
1926	John C. Miles, Sydney Mines, Nova Scotia	2:25:40	1959	Eino Oksanen, Finland	2:22:42
1927	Clarence DeMar, Melrose, MA	2:40:22	1960	Paavo Kotila, Finland	2:20:54
1928	Clarence DeMar, Melrose, MA	2:37:07	1961	Eino Oksanen, Finland	2:23:39
1929	John C. Miles, Hamilton, Ontario	2:33:08	1962	Eino Oksanen, Finland	2:23:48

1963	Aurele Vandendriessche, Belgium	2:18:58
1964	Aurele Vandendriessche, Belgium	2:19:59
1965	Morio Shigematsu, Japan	2:16:33
1966	Kenji Kimihara, Japan	2:17:11
1967	David McKenzie, New Zealand	2:15:45
1968	Ambrose (Amby) Burfoot, Groton, CT	2:22:17
1969	Yoshiaki Unetani, Japan	2:13:49
1970	Ron Hill, England	2:10:30
1971	Alvaro Mejia, Columbia	2:18:45
1972	Olavi Suomalainen, Finland	2:15:39
1973	Jon Anderson, Eugene, OR	2:16:03
1974	Neil Cusack, Ireland	2:13:39
1975	Bill Rodgers, Melrose, MA	2:09:55
1976	Jack Fultz, Arlington, VA	2:20:19
1977	Jerome Drayton, Toronto, Ontario	2:14:46
1978	Bill Rodgers, Melrose, MA	2:10:13
1979	Bill Rodgers, Melrose, MA	2:09:27
1980	Bill Rodgers, Melrose, MA	2:12:11
1981	Toshihiko Seko, Japan	2:09:26
1982	Alberto Salazar, Wayland, MA	2:08:52
1983	Gregory A. Meyer, Wellesley, MA	2:09:00
1984	Geoff Smith, England	2:10:34
1985	Geoff Smith, England	2:14:05
1986	Rob de Castella, Australia	2:07:51
1987	Toshihiko Seko, Japan	2:11:50
1988	Ibrahim Hussein, Kenya	2:08:43
1989	Abebe Mekonnen, Ethiopia	2:09:06
1990	Gelindo Bordin, Italy	2:08:19
1991	Ibrahim Hussein, Kenya	2:11:06
1992	Ibrahim Hussein, Kenya	2:08:14
1993	Cosmas Ndeti, Kenya	2:09:33
1994	Cosmas Ndeti, Kenya	2:07:15
1995	Cosmas Ndeti, Kenya	2:09:22
1996	Moses Tanui, Kenya	2:09:26
1997	Lameck Aguta, Kenya	2:10:34

WOMEN'S OPEN CHAMPIONS

YEAR	NAME/RESIDENCE	TIME
1966	Roberta Gibb, Winchester, MA	3:21:40 *
1967	Roberta Gibb, San Diego, CA	3:27:17 *
1968	Roberta Gibb, San Diego, CA	3:30:00 *
1969	Sara Mae Berman, Cambridge, MA	3:22:46 *
1970	Sara Mae Berman, Cambridge, MA	3:05:07 *
1971	Sara Mae Berman, Cambridge, MA	3:08:30 *
1972	Nina Kuscsik, South Huntington, NY	3:10:26
1973	Jacqueline Hansen, Granada Hills, CA	3:05:59
1974	Michiko Gorman, Los Angeles, CA	2:47:11
1975	Liane Winter, West Germany	2:42:24
1976	Kim Merritt, Kenosha, WI	2:47:10
1977	Michiko Gorman, Los Angeles, CA	2:48:33
1978	Gayle Barron, Atlanta, GA	2:44:52
1979	Joan Benoit, Cape Elizabeth, ME	2:35:15
1980	Jacqueline Gareau, Montreal, Quebec	2:34:28
1981	Allison Roe, New Zealand	2:26:46
1982	Charlotte Teske, West Germany	2:29:33
1983	Joan Benoit, Watertown, MA	2:22:43
1984	Lorraine Moeller, New Zealand	2:29:28
1985	Lisa Larsen Weidenbach, Battle Creek, MI	2:34:06
1986	Ingrid Kristiansen, Norway	2:24:55
1987	Rosa Mota, Portugal	2:25:21
1988	Rosa Mota, Portugal	2:24:30
1989	Ingrid Kristiansen, Norway	2:24:33
1990	Rosa Mota, Portugal	2:25:24
1991	Wanda Panfil, Poland	2:24:18
1992	Olga Markova, Russia	2:23:43
1993	Olga Markova, Russia	2:25:27
1994	Uta Pippig, Germany	2:21:45
1995	Uta Pippig, Germany	2:25:11
1996	Uta Pippig, Germany	2:27:12
1997	Fatuma Roba, Ethiopia	2:26:23

MEN'S WHEELCHAIR CHAMPIONS

YEAR	NAME/RESIDENCE	TIME
1970	Eugene Roberts, Baltimore, MD	8:00:00
1975	Robert Hall, Belmont, MA	2:58:00
1976	No contestants	
1977	Robert Hall, Belmont, MA	2:40:10
1978	George Murray, Tampa, FL	2:26:57
1979	Kenneth Archer, Akron, OH	2:38:59
1980	Curt Brinkman, Orem, UT	1:55:00
1981	Jim Martinson, Puyallup, WA	2:00:41
1982	Jim Knaub, Long Beach, CA	1:51:31
1983	Jim Knaub, Long Beach, CA	1:47:10
1984	Andre Viger, Quebec, Canada	2:05:20
1985	George Murray, Tampa, FL	1:45:34
1986	Andre Viger, Quebec, Canada	1:43:25
1987	Andre Viger, Quebec, Canada	1:55:42
1988	Mustapha Badid, France	1:43:19
1989	Philippe Couprie, France	1:36:04
1990	Mustapha Badid, France	1:29:53
1991	Jim Knaub, Long Beach, CA	1:30:44
1992	Jim Knaub, Long Beach, CA	1:26:28
1993	Jim Knaub, Long Beach, CA	1:22:17
1994	Heinz Frei, Switzerland	1:21:23
1995	Franz Nietlispach, Switzerland	1:25:59
1996	Heinz Frei, Switzerland	1:30:14
1997	Franz Nietlispach, Switzerland	1:28:14

WOMEN'S WHEELCHAIR CHAMPIONS

YEAR	NAME/RESIDENCE	TIME
1977	Sharon Rahn, Champaign, IL	3:48:51
1978	Susan Schapiro, Berkeley, CA	3:52:35
1979	Sheryl Bair, Sacramento, CA	3:27:56
1980	Sharon Limpert, Minneapolis, MN	2:49:04
1981	Candace Cable, Las Vegas, NV	2:38:41
1982	Candace Cable-Brookes, Las Vegas, NV	2:12:43
1983	Sherry Ramsey, Arvada, CO	2:27:07
1984	Sherry Ramsey, Arvada, CO	2:56:51
1985	Candace Cable-Brookes, Long Beach, CA	2:05:26
1986	Candace Cable-Brookes, Long Beach, CA	2:09:28
1987	Candace Cable-Brookes, Long Beach, CA	2:19:55
1988	Candace Cable-Brookes, Long Beach, CA	2:10:44
1989	Connie Hansen, Denmark	1:50:06
1990	Jean Driscoll, Champagne, IL	1:43:17
1991	Jean Driscoll, Champagne, IL	1:42:42
1992	Jean Driscoll, Champagne, IL	1:36:52
1993	Jean Driscoll, Champagne, IL	1:34:50
1994	Jean Driscoll, Champagne, IL	1:34:22
1995	Jean Driscoll, Champagne, IL	1:40:42
1996	Jean Driscoll, Champagne, IL	1:52:56
1997	Louise Sauvage, Australia	1:54:28

BIBLIOGRAPHY

BOOKS

Benoit-Samuelson, Joan & Baker, Sally. *Running Tide.* New York: Alfred Knopf, 1987

Benyo, Richard. *The Masters of the Marathon.* New York: Atheneum, 1983

Curtis, John Gould. *History of Brookline.* Boston: Houghton Mifflin, 1933

Daniels, John. *In Freedom's Birthplace, A Story of Boston's Negroes.* Boston: Houghton Mifflin, 1914

Derderian, Tom. *Boston Marathon—The History of the World's Premier Running Event.* Champaign, IL: Human Kinetics, 1994

Falls, Joe. *The Boston Marathon.* New York: MacMillan Publishing, 1977

Higdon, Hal. *A Century of Running Boston.* Emmaus, PA: Rodale Press, 1995

Hinchcliffe, Elizabeth. *Five Pounds Currency—Three Pounds of Corn—The Wellesley Centennial Story.* Wellesley, 1981

Homer, Joel. *Marathons—The Ultimate Challenge.* Garden City, NY: Dolphin Books-Doubleday, 1979

Hosler, Ray. *Boston—America's Oldest Marathon.* Mountain View, CA: Anderson World, Inc., 1980

Kardong, Don. *Thirty Phone Booths to Boston—Tales of the Wayward Runner.* NY: MacMillan, 1985

Lewis, Frederick & Johnson, Dick. *Young at Heart.* Waco, TX: WRS Publishing, 1992

Natick Federal Savings & Loan Associates. *The Story of Natick.* Natick, MA: Suburban Press, 1948

Rodgers, Bill & Concannon, Joe. *Marathoning.* NY: Simon & Schuster, 1980

Stafford, Francis A. *Brief History of Hopkinton.* 1915

Temple, Josiah H. *History of Framingham, Massachusetts, 1640-1885.* Framingham, MA: 1988

PERIODICALS

Accomplishments of Henry Wilson-1993

A Social & Architectural History of 19th Century Natick, Massachusetts-1988

Boston Athletic Association Program-1996

Boston College Magazine-1996

History of the Boston Public Library-March, 1987

Massachusetts Municipal Profiles-1994–1995

Middlesex News-1980–1997

Natick Bulletin & Sun-March 17, 1983

Newton Registry-1896

Runners World-1997

Sports Illustrated-September 16, 1996

The Boston Globe-1896–1997

The Boston Herald (Traveler)–1950–1997

The Magazine of History, Vol. XII-February, 1911

The Paper-April 18, 1973

INDEX

Page numbers in italics represent illustrations.

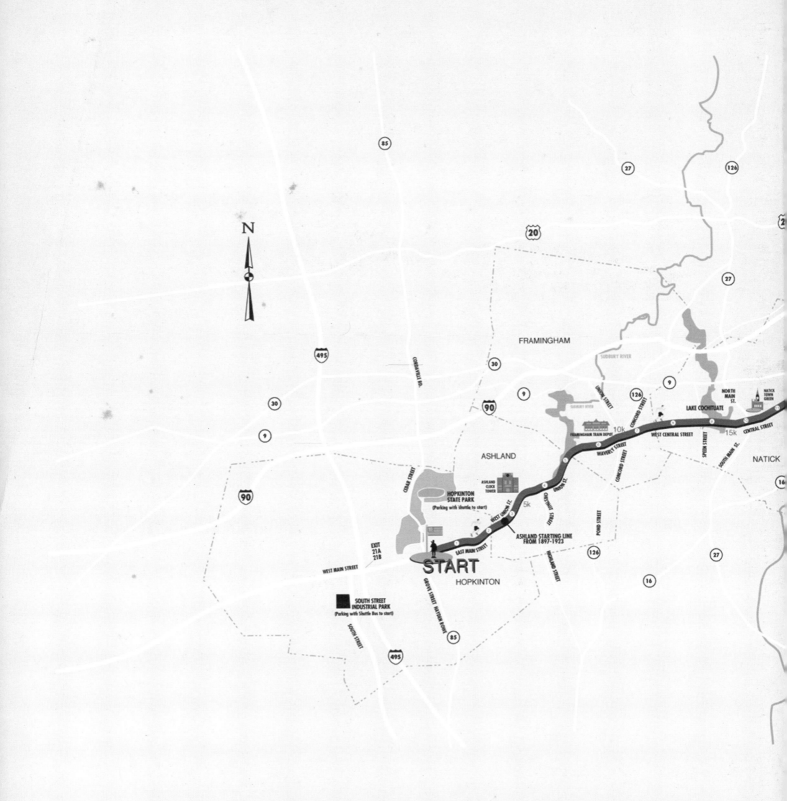